Diane + Bob,
See p. 115. It is possible that the stained glass window in the observatory is Tiffany — see the similarities in the signed pieces in N.J. You may want to check this out when you have the time.
John

THE EAST COAST
BED &
BREAKFAST
GUIDE

Breakfast at Heatherlea, Philadelphia, Pennsylvania

THE EAST COAST
BED &
BREAKFAST
GUIDE
NEW ENGLAND AND
THE MID-ATLANTIC

BY ROBERTA GARDNER

Photographs by George W. Gardner

DESIGNED AND PRODUCED BY
ROBERT R. REID
AND
TERRY BERGER

SIMON AND SCHUSTER
NEW YORK

FRONT COVER PHOTOGRAPH:
  The Beal House Inn, Littleton, New Hampshire
FRONTISPIECE PHOTOGRAPH:
  1811 House, Manchester Center, Vermont
COUNTRY SPREAD, PAGES 44–45:
  Amish farmer en route to market near Intercourse, Pennsylvania

Editorial assistance by Christine Timmons
  and Jim Carnes
Map by Anthony St. Aubyn

The photographs on pages 26, 94, and 95 are by Will Fowler.

Published by Simon and Schuster
A Division of Simon & Schuster, Inc.
Simon & Schuster Building
Rockefeller Center
1230 Avenue of the Americas
New York, New York 10020
SIMON AND SCHUSTER and colophon are registered trademarks of Simon & Schuster, Inc.

A Robert Reid/Terry Berger production
Typeset in Bodoni Book by Monotype Composition Company, Baltimore
Printed and bound by Mandarin Offset International, Ltd., Hong Kong

1 2 3 4 5 6 7 8 9 10

Library of Congress Cataloging in Publication Data

Gardner, Roberta Homan.
  The East Coast bed & breakfast guide.

  1. Hotels, taverns, etc.—New England—Directories.
2. Hotels, taverns, etc.—Middle Atlantic States—'
Directories.   I. Title.   II. Title: East Coast bed and
breakfast guide.   III. Title: Bed & breakfast guide.
IV. Title: Bed and breakfast guide.
TX907.G33 1984   647'.9474   84-10699

ISBN 0-671-50845-8

CONTENTS

Bed & Breakfast in the City

Bed & Breakfast in the Country

NOTE: all the cities and towns on this map contain
the bed and breakfasts described in this book.

ME

Bar Harbor

ebunkport

rovincetown

rnstable

AUTHOR'S NOTE

Americans are quickly discovering the charm, adventure, romance, good value, and personal attention that typify bed and breakfast travel. Opportunities to form new friendships and to find camaraderie with both hosts and guests present themselves in a setting of relaxed intimacy.

To make a visit most successful, we offer the following tips:

• Cancellations are difficult for places with a limited number of guest rooms.

• If your arrival will be delayed, call your host just as you would a friend who was expecting you.

• Adhere to the policy regarding smoking, children, and pets.

• Remember that you are in someone's home, and that mutual kindness and respect and general consideration will enhance the bed and breakfast experience.

OVERLEAF: *the aerial tram to Roosevelt Island affords a stunning, five-minute view of Manhattan's skyline. Running alongside, the Queensboro 59th Street bridge spans the East River at this point.*

BED & BREAKFAST
IN THE CITY

BOSTON

"The cradle of American Independence"

The capital city of New England, contemporary Boston is a mosaic of history, education, and culture. Dubbed "the cradle of American Independence," it was here that the colonists fomented a rebellion that cocked the trigger of the American Revolution. Most famous among these incendiary acts was the Boston Tea Party. Revolting against the British tax on tea, ninety colonists dressed as Indians boarded three East India Company ships and dumped their entire cargo of tea overboard. England reacted by closing the port, which, in turn, precipitated the organization of the minutemen. The rest is history.

Founded by Puritans in 1630, Boston retains in its contemporary character strains of its Puritan roots. Foremost among its Puritan principles was the establishment of a sound educational system.

Today, Boston is the leading city of American education, sheltering approximately fifty colleges and universities, including Harvard, the first college in the colonies, founded in 1636. A vast population of students adds a bouyant and youthful zest to this otherwise staid city.

As early as the 1800s, Boston was known as the "Athens of America"; the city attracted intellectuals and writers, and inspired philanthropy. As a result, Boston is home to a distinguished symphony orchestra and first-rate opera company, and it is filled with wonderful museums. Most notable of these is the Boston Museum of Fine Arts, which contains superb collections, particularly in the areas of Asian, Egyptian, and classical arts.

Boston would not be Boston without the Irish, who wield power in the political arena, and the Italians, whose neighborhood in the North End is filled with colorful cafés, markets, and restaurants. One of the first American cities to revitalize its blighted neighborhoods, Boston prides itself on Faneuil Hall Marketplace, the lively commercial center along the waterfront and the showcase of this movement.

Left, The Boston Museum of Fine Arts, and its superb Asian collection, above.

A beehive fireplace, original to the oldest part of the house.

MEDFORD

An 18th-century architectural jewel

Seven miles from the center of Boston, this large, eighteenth-century home is an architectural gem. The original section of the house was built circa 1720, and detailing, such as two-panel doors, vertical plank walls with hair plaster, and original hand-wrought hardware, remains intact. By 1799 the house changed hands, and its wealthy new owner undertook a major renovation in the Federal style. A few of the fine details reflecting that period are twelve-over-twelve window sashes with a number of original, Crown glass panes, spackle-painted floors, and fine mantels and doors. The breakfast room—a contemporary addition—opens onto a slate patio and formal gardens that guests enjoy during warm months of the year.

MEDFORD. Eighteenth-century home that retains its original beehive hearth. Open year-round. Two guest rooms, shared bath. Rates: $40 single, $50 double. Continental breakfast. No pets; no smoking. In residential neighborhood, close to Tufts University and 15 minutes from downtown Boston. *Represented by Bed and Breakfast Associates, Bay Colony Ltd., Boston, MA.*

SOUTH END

A brick townhouse on a restored street

The gentrified South End of Boston is home to this 1881 bow-front brick townhouse on one of the beautifully restored streets of the St. Botolph area. Owned by a vivacious, outgoing professional couple, the townhouse enjoys special architectural features that include brownstone steps and exquisite stained-glass windows. From this vantage point, Symphony Hall, Copley Plaza, and the Prudential Center are an easy walk.

SOUTH END. Brick bow-front, 1881 brownstone. Open year-round. Two guest rooms, shared bath. Rates: $38 to $50 single, $55 to $60 double; $10 for third person. No children under ten; no pets; no smoking. In St. Botolph neighborhood, within walking distance of downtown Boston. *Represented by Bed and Breakfast Associates, Bay Colony, Ltd., Boston, MA.*

Your own private studio.

The light-bejeweled entryway.

SOUTH END

The top floor of a private townhouse

Along the perimeter of the South End renovation are several streets that reflect both the "before" and "after." Experienced urban dwellers may be more accustomed to the uneven quality of the neighborhood, but even the most fastidious will be delighted to stay in this private studio apartment, the top floor of a private townhouse. Soon to be completed is an adjoining city park, which will make the Prudential Center easily accessible by foot.

SOUTH END. Brick townhouse, built in 1870. Open year-round. Studio apartment with fully equipped kitchen and private bath. Rates: $60 per night. Fixings provided for guests to prepare full breakfast. In older, mixed neighborhood, close to museums and transportation. *Represented by Bed and Breakfast Associates, Bay Colony Ltd., Boston, MA.*

BACK BAY

On one of the loveliest streets in Boston

Designed with an impressive slate entry hall, thirteen-foot coffered ceiling, wrought-iron staircase, and heavy carved doors, the Spanish-style interior of this massive double townhouse belies its locale, which is pure Yankee. Equidistant from the hurly burly of Newbury Street and Copley Plaza, and the genteel charms of Beacon Hill, this bed and breakfast is situated on one of the loveliest streets in Boston.

BACK BAY. Brick home with 13-foot coffered ceilings and interesting interior. Open year-round. One guest room, shared bath. Rates: $45 to $55 single, $55 to $65 double. Continental breakfast. No children under thirteen; no pets. On a lovely street in the Back Bay neighborhood, close to Boston Common and downtown Boston. *Represented by Bed and Breakfast Associates, Bay Colony Ltd., Boston, MA.*

Living room, above, and the sunlit breakfast room, right.

High ceilings create wonderful spaces.

BACK BAY

A penthouse near Boston Common

Two blocks from the Boston Common and the charming swan boats of the Public Garden, and likewise close to the boutiques and shops lining Newbury Street, this fourth-floor Back Bay penthouse apartment is blessed with well-proportioned rooms lit by a skylight, and a spacious roof deck. Here, guests may while away the time soaking in the morning sun with a mug of bracing coffee or tea, or enjoying an impromptu picnic lunch overlooking the historic rooftops of Boston.

BACK BAY. Brownstone built in 1878, with fourth-floor, walk-up penthouse. Open year-round, except for occasional vacations. One guest room, private bath close by. Rates: $55 single, $60 double; $5 surcharge for one-night stay. Continental breakfast. No facilities for infants; no pets; no smoking. In the heart of Boston, 2 blocks from Boston Common. *Represented by Bed and Breakfast Associates, Bay Colony Ltd., Boston, MA.*

NEW YORK

"I'll take Manhattan

Only 13.4 miles long and 2.3 miles wide at its broadest point, Manhattan is more a complex world than a city. Contrast is at the very heart of its nature. Though it is populated by immigrants, it embodies a quintessentially American spirit. It is simultaneously cynical and soft-hearted, completely cosmopolitan and just as completely loyal to neighborhood, race, and culture. Not a take-it-or-leave-it town, it repels people as often as it attracts them.

One of the most enjoyable and educational introductions to Manhattan is a tour of the island from its surrounding waters, via a Circle Line boat. Employing a combination of history, humor, and encyclopedic knowledge, Circle Line guides succinctly sum up the city in a short three hours. Another classic method of getting a feel for the geography of the metropolis is to scale the heights of the Empire State Building or its more recent counterparts, the World Trade Towers. From this dizzying perspective, the layout of the city is revealed by day. By night Manhattan offers a gamut of entertainments to suit every taste: from ballroom dancing and disco, smoky jazz clubs and posh supper clubs, to Broadway shows and New Wave performance art.

and Long Island too"

Justifiably famous for its potatoes, ducks, and bay scallops, the choicest part of Long Island for most visitors is the Hamptons, which consist of seven villages at the eastern tip of the island. Founded by Puritans, the Hamptons are mostly populated today by writers, artists, and the rich— surrounded by historic sites, elegant mansions, respected galleries, and the choicest of shops. The Marine Museum in nearby Amagansett and Sag Harbor's Whaling Museum offer relics of the island's nineteenth-century whaling days, and a ferry from Sag Harbor to Shelter Island will bring you to miles of white sand beaches. In Montauk, the island's most eastern point, the lighthouse was commissioned by George Washington in 1795. Finally, there is the famous Fire Island, off the south shore, where commercialism is discouraged to ensure an unspoiled retreat from modern life.

Left, busy Grand Central Terminal on 42nd Street. Above, the magnetic arch at Washington Square.

GREENWICH VILLAGE

A luxuriously converted warehouse

Greenwich Village has a reputation for harboring nonconformists and artists. Its crooked streets are filled with restaurants, theaters, and cafés as well as jazz, folk, and rock clubs. It attracts seekers of low-key nightlife. Yet the Village remains a neighborhood that feels manageable and cozy. Besides its proximity to all the Village diversions, this beautifully appointed apartment is within walking distance of Soho, Little Italy, and Chinatown.

GREENWICH VILLAGE. Attractive conversion of an old warehouse into living quarters with modern décor. Open year-round. One guest room, or occasionally the entire apartment, comprising a living room, dining area, full kitchen, sleeping loft, bedroom, and bath. Rates $40 single, $55 double, two-night minimum; $110 entire apartment per night. Continental breakfast, or guests may prepare full breakfast. No pets; no smoking. Close to N.Y.U. and Washington Square. *Represented by The B&B Group (New Yorkers at Home), Inc.New York City.*

Vintage furnishings and a kosher kitchen.

Left, a sleeping gallery for the more adventurous, or a sumptuous master bedroom, above.

ROOSEVELT ISLAND

A stunning view of Manhattan's skyline

Linked to the "big island" by an aerial tramway across the East River, tiny Roosevelt Island (2½ miles long and 800 feet wide) is a "town-in-town"; a three-minute ride to the city but a world removed. The community houses over two thousand familes as well as retail shops, two city hospitals, parks, and a pre-Revolutionary landmark, Blackwell Farmhouse.

Even a Manhattanite might be tempted to spend a night at this two-story apartment. Its wall of glass faces onto the river, offering an unparalleled view of the skyline.

ROOSEVELT ISLAND. Three-story contemporary apartment building with panoramic view of Manhattan and the East River. Open year-round. Two guest rooms, shared bath. Rates: $40 single, $55 double. Continental breakfast (kosher kitchen). Children over eight; no pets. Represented by *The B & B Group (New Yorkers at Home) Inc., NYC.*

UPPER EAST SIDE

Three short blocks from Bloomingdale's

This apartment on the East Side of Manhattan is just three short blocks from Bloomingdale's department store. The neighborhood is chock-a-block with chic shops, restaurants, movie theaters, and discothèques. Also, from Midtown it is relatively easy to travel to any other part of the city. The apartment's eclectic collection of antique furnishings and period pieces is dramatic and interesting. The guest bedroom is large enough to include a reading nook.

UPPER EAST SIDE. Antiques-furnished apartment in high-rise building. One guest room with private bath. Rates: $45 single, $55 double. Continental breakfast. *Represented by The B & B Group (New Yorkers at Home) Inc., NYC.*

Brownstone peace and tranquillity, above. An exotic breakfast setting, right.

UPPER WEST SIDE

Spacious brownstone in a dynamic area

A sense of spaciousness comes from the fact that this three-story brownstone townhouse is a single-family dwelling. The third floor guest rooms were once the children's bedrooms and retain souvenirs of their adolescence. Just off Columbus Avenue—the most up and coming neighborhood in Manhattan—guests are close to Central Park, the American Museum of Natural History, and Lincoln Center as well as a plethora of fascinating shops and wonderful restaurants.

UPPER WEST SIDE. Brownstone and brick townhouse, built in 1887, with goldfish pond in back yard. Open mid-September through May (closed during Christmas). Three guest rooms, shared bath. Rates: $38 singles, $50 double. Continental breakfast. No children under twelve, no pets; smoking discouraged. Close to Lincoln Center and Columbus Avenue. *Represented by Urban Ventures, Inc., New York City.*

An intricately carved pier glass.

Hostess Wendy Berry in her kitchen.

UPPER WEST SIDE

Cooking classes on Wednesday nights

If you arrive on a Wednesday night, you might partake of one of Wendy Berry's cooking classes which convene in her tiny apartment kitchen. A caterer and photographer, Wendy also works for New York's Board of Education. Her two-level apartment in a large and elegant brownstone is located on a tree-lined street on the Upper West Side. Just a block from Columbus Avenue, the neighborhood is fast becoming a haven for young professionals. This influx of the upwardly mobile has triggered a renaissance; the Upper West Side has blossomed into the most dynamic neighborhood in all of Manhattan. Every day new restaurants, fabulous food emporiums, and trendy boutiques appear, replacing the down-at-the-heels businesses that characterized the Columbus Avenue of yesterday.

UPPER WEST SIDE. Two-level apartment in brownstone townhouse. Open year-round. One guest room, shared bath. Rates: $40 single, $55 double. Continental breakfast. No children under twelve; no pets; no smoking. In Upper West Side neighborhood with endless possibilities for entertainment. Represented by *The B & B Group (New Yorkers at Home) Inc., NYC.*

EAST HAMPTON

Private decks and modern luxury

East Hampton is a colonial town complete with village green, windmill , and a three-century-old cemetery. Surrounded by gently rolling hills, the area is conducive to quiet activities: walks on the beach, candlelight dinners, reading.

This contemporary cottage is nestled in the treetops, along a quiet lane just outside of town. Its natural siding blends with the landscape, and each room has a private deck and entrance of its own. With the perfect home from which to start the business, these hosts operate the bed and breakfast reservation service, Alternate Lodgings.

EAST HAMPTON. Contemporary home with floor-to-ceiling windows in the living room and a treetop deck. Open April through October. Three guest rooms, private and shared baths. Rates: $65 to $75 double. Continental breakfast daily, often full breakfast on Sunday. No children; no pets; Visa/MasterCard/ American Express. *Represented by Alternate Lodgings, Inc., East Hampton, NY.*

Each luxurious guest room has a private entrance.

SOUTHAMPTON

A beach cottage, smart pubs, discos

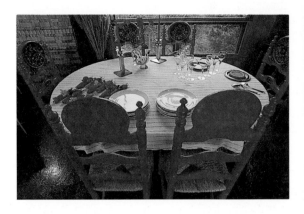

The elegant summer cottages that line the beach at Southampton bespeak the days when this was mecca for the very wealthy. Though socialites are still in evidence, young professionals and jet-setters are giving new energy to the town. Home of Job's Lane, the Hampton's most prestigious shopping district, Southampton also nurtures a thriving social life and by night, comes alive with pubs and discos.

Outside of town, this secluded beach house has a sauna, a private beach with dock, and a wraparound deck with views of the water.

SOUTHAMPTON. Contemporary home in wooded setting, over-looking the ocean. Open year-round. Three guest rooms (all with twins), shared and private baths. Rates: $65 double. Continental breakfast. No children; no pets. Sauna and private beach with dock. *Represented by Alternate Lodgings, Inc., East Hampton, NY.*

Modern luxury and an ocean view.

Casual elegance on chic Long Island.

AMAGANSETT

Bluejeans and tennis shoes

"If I were asked what to pack for a stay in Amagansett, I would suggest blue jeans and tennis shoes," observes a life-long resident of the area. An artists' enclave for many years, this is one of the quietest of the Hampton's beach communities, though several of the beautiful town beaches do attract a singles crowd.

Along a sandy lane, walking distance to the beach, this home is the casually elegant, year-round residence of two New York City professionals.

AMAGANSETT. New England-style colonial home with private beach. Open year-round. One guest room, private bath. Rates $65 double. Continental or full breakfast available. No children; no pets; smoking discouraged. Within walking distance of the ocean; summer stock, fishing, sailing, excellent dining nearby. *Represented by Alternate Lodgings, Inc., East Hampton, NY.*

PHILADELPHIA

Preserves the old, nourishes the new

In the late 1600s, Thomas Holme designed the colonial city of Philadelphia in a simple grid pattern. Bounded on the east by the Delaware River, the site of founder William Penn's landing in 1682, the entire city then encompassed two square miles. Contemporary "historic Philadelphia" is a vital neighborhood surrounded by a sprawling city of neighborhoods; it shelters the old and nourishes the new. At the center of the grid resides the Liberty Bell and Independence Hall, where the Second Continental Congress met, the Declaration of Independence was signed, and the Constitution of the United States was drafted. Travel east to the river and find New-Market and Head House Square—the popular multi-level complex of *au courant* boutiques and restaurants, and an open-air market; the rejuvenated neighborhoods of Queen Village, Society Hill, and Old City; and the esplanades and marina at Penn's Landing.

A neighborhood of towering Victorian row houses just west of the historic city center, University City is named for its proximity to the University of Pennsylvania and Drexel University.

The Spring Garden district, along the northern border of the historic area, is the center for the arts. Anyone who saw the movie *Rocky* can visualize the steps that lead to the Philadelphia Museum of Art. The Rodin Museum, the Academy of Natural Sciences, and the gateway to Fairmount Park are found in this neighborhood. Fairmount Park, with 8,700 total acres, is the largest city park in the world and contains the Philadelphia Zoo; the home and garden of John Bartram, the first American botanist; Boat House Row; and the Playhouse in the Park.

Intertwined with these major neighborhoods are the Italian Market, dozens of small museums and eighteenth-century homes, the U.S. Mint, thirteen colonial churches, a Revolutionary fort, and other noteworthy and historic sites. Exploring Philadelphia could consume a lifetime.

Left, William Penn stands tall atop the city hall in Philadelphia, where no building can be built higher than him. Above, Boathouse Row, where ten rowing clubs light up their nineteenth-century boathouses on the Schuylkill River.

Left, your sitting room, dogs not included, and one of two bedrooms, above.

CHESTER COUNTY

A gristmill in foxhunting country

One of the most atmospheric landscapes in the mid-Atlantic, the rolling hills of the Brandywine Valley are interspersed with charming stone houses and covered bridges. This rustic gristmill, built around 1750, has been converted into spacious living quarters, complete with first-floor stables that house the owner's two horses. Besides enjoying the gentle beauty of Chester County, guests may follow fox hunts, for which the area is famous.

CHESTER COUNTY. Eighteenth-century gristmill converted into a residence in 1946. Open year-round. Two guest rooms, shared bath. Rates: $35 single, $45 double. Full breakfast. Pets accepted; can accommodate 2 horses in winter, 4 in summer. Forty minutes from Pennsylvania Dutch country; weekly fox hunts; Longwood Gardens, Winterthur Museum nearby. *Represented by Bed and Breakfast of Philadelphia, Philadelphia, PA.*

Room in which to spread out and relax

A grandly proportioned Queen Anne-style townhouse, this bed and breakfast home gives guests room to spread out and really relax. The bedroom is large enough to easily handle two couches, two chairs, and a double bed and still leave lots of floor space. A television, radio, and a working fireplace, flanked by built-in bookcases, complete the room. One especially thoughtful touch is the electric coffeepot, filled and ready to go, just outside the door.

UNIVERSITY CITY. Queen Anne Victorian townhouse. Open year-round. One guest room, shared bath. Rates: $35 single, $40 double. Hearty continental breakfast served daily, full breakfast available on weekends. No pets. Near Civic Center; all of Philadelphia easily accessible. *Represented by Bed & Breakfast of Philadelphia, Philadelphia, PA.*

An original Eames chair in the guest room.

Entry hall to the spacious rooms.

Federal townhouse near Society Hill

Poised between Society Hill and NewMarket, visitors to the newly restored areas of "historic Philadelphia" couldn't ask for a more convenient location. Meticulously renovated, this 1811 Federal townhouse beautifully weds mellow woodwork, exposed beams and brickwork, a pine floor, and working fireplaces with contemporary furnishings. The popular NewMarket shopping and dining complex is visible through the French doors in the guest bedroom.

NEWMARKET. Federal-style home built in 1811, with contemporary décor. Open year-round. One guest room, private bath. Rates: $30 single, $40 double. Hearty continental breakfast; guests may prepare full breakfast if they wish. No children; no pets. In NewMarket area, within walking distance of the historic district. *Represented by Bed & Breakfast of Philadelphia, Philadelphia, PA.*

SPRING GARDEN

Near the Museum of Art

The owner of this home is a dedicated collector of American antiques. His century-old townhouse, just six blocks from the Philadelphia Museum of Art, contains a fine collection of museum-quality artifacts. The first-floor living room displays such treasures as a Shaker child's chair, a Pennsylvania farm bench with original decorative paint, and Hudson River School paintings. Bedrooms are decorated with pre-Revolutionary pewter, jacquard coverlets and Sabbath Day Lake four-slat rockers.

SPRING GARDEN. Simple townhouse built in 1856 and largely furnished with American antiques. Open year-round. Two guest rooms, shared bath. Rates: $35 single, $45 double. Full breakfast (prepared by guests during the week). No children; no pets. In Spring Garden district, near museums and Fairmount Park. *Represented by Bed & Breakfast of Philadelphia, Philadelphia, PA.*

Roughing it, Philadelphia style.

NORTH PHILADELPHIA

A back-garden greenhouse becomes a fantasy cottage

Decorated with a light and casual hand, this combination greenhouse-and-potting-shed cottage is so inviting that many guests simply disappear for days on end, succumbing to the intimacy of the setting. The cottage shares a broad expanse of lawn with the main house and is bordered on one side by a picturesque grape arbor, and on the other by a large swimming pool. Only twenty-five minutes from Center City, this fantasy cottage is an ideal romantic getaway.

NORTH PHILADELPHIA. Private cottage, a combination greenhouse and potting shed, on three acres. Open year-round. One guest room (the potting shed), private bath (greenhouse). Rates: $55 one or two people. Continental breakfast can be fixed from ample supplies in refrigerator. No facilities for young children; inquire about pets. Swimming pool on premises; stable, tennis, golf nearby. *Represented by Bed & Breakfast of Philadelphia, Philadelphia, PA.*

An antiques collection on permanent display.

Left, one of two charming bedrooms displays a wall hanging made by the hostess. Above, the formal dining room is used for breakfast.

THE MAIN LINE

An impressive estate

A solid and impressive Main Line estate, Heatherlea was built in 1890 for a prominent Philadelphia family. Visitors luxuriate in the privacy of the third floor and enjoy impeccably decorated, antiques-filled bedrooms, which display well-executed needlepoint wall-hangings and pillows, all designed by the hostess. After a full breakfast in the formal dining room, guests may repair to the Jacuzzi or swimming pool. Sheltered by the privacy of ample, tree-shaded grounds, this is the perfect place to unwind.

THE MAIN LINE. "Heatherlea," an elegant Greek Revival summer home, built in 1890. Open year-round. Two guest rooms and one suite with two bedrooms; shared bath. Rates: $40 single, $50 double. Varied breakfast menu changes daily. No pets. Never takes two parties who don't know each other. Pool in backyard, tennis and golf nearby; ½-hour drive from Philadelphia. *Represented by Bed & Breakfast of Philadelphia, Philadelphia, PA.*

BALTIMORE

The Miracle of Rebirth

It would be worthwhile to visit Baltimore if only to observe a venerable American city undergoing the miracle of rebirth. The seed for this resurgence was sown in 1954 when city merchants banded together to staunch the flow of revenue from the city to the suburbs and beyond. The momentum built slowly over the next twenty-five years, and under the leadership of Baltimore's dynamic mayor, William Donald Schaefer, the city has been changing daily and surging forward. Abandoned neighborhoods are being reclaimed; imagination is hard at work.

Nowhere is the renaissance of Baltimore more apparent than at the Inner Harbor, which glitters at its heart. Designed to make the best use of the city's snug waterfront, the immediate area is comprised of the thirty-story World Trade Center, The National Aquarium at Baltimore, the U.S.F. *Constellation*, and two contemporary glass pavil-

ions called Harborplace, all connected by a charming brick promenade.

The two "crystal palace" pavilions serve different purposes. The Pratt Street Pavilion is occupied by full-service ethnic and seafood restaurants and specialty shops, which carry everything from clothing and candy to kitchenware and kites. The adjacent Food Palace pavilion is, as the name suggests, a haven of casual foods that can be eaten at stand-up tables inside, or on the portico overlooking the harbor. From this vantage point, visitors enjoy the impromptu entertainments—magicians, mimes, musicians—that take place year-round on the promenade.

After quelling hunger pangs and before purchasing take-home gifts, visitors should tour the U.S. frigate *Constellation*—the first ship of the U.S. Navy, launched in 1797. Afterwards, spend a spellbound hour in the aquarium. Built at the tip of Pier Three, this dramatic yet graceful building juts out into the water, its triangulated glass roof pointing straight up into the sky. The aquarium's five levels contain a huge coral reef, a walk-through rain forest, and many fascinating smaller exhibits.

Left, above, the Inner Harbor, showing the U.S.F. Constellation *and I. M. Pei's World Trade Building. Left, below, the wonderful new Aquarium. Above, the inside of the Food Palace.*

PRINCE OF WALES INN

Elegant, small hotel near the harbor

The birth of the Prince of Wales Inn is part of the rebirth of Baltimore. In 1982, interior designer Mary Glick bought a neglected, century-old townhouse—which sits across from Saint Elizabeth Ann Seton's home and neighboring St. Mary's Seminary—and restored it to life, an accomplishment that won her the 1983 Restoration of the Year award from the Baltimore Heritage.

The first bed and breakfast inn in the city, The Prince of Wales feels both like an elegant small hotel and a real part of the energy that is powering Baltimore's renaissance. Each of the four guest rooms in the main house and the two, fully equipped apartments on the rear courtyard are tastefully decorated with elegant draperies, thick plush carpeting, excellent traditional furnishings, lamps of cut glass or Oriental porcelain, comfortable beds, and wonderful vanity lights in the bathrooms.

Breakfast is served in the first-floor dining room and can be transported to the open-air courtyard or to the front parlor, which is simply furnished with brocade chairs and couch, an Oriental rug, and silk flower arrangements. Innkeeper Jennifer Glick, Mary's daughter, serves an "expanded" continental breakfast, which includes cheese, hard-cooked eggs, cereals, freshly baked breads, and juices. If you specify a time, Jennifer will place a thermos of tea or coffee in a basket outside your door in the morning as a welcome eye-opener.

PRINCE OF WALES INN, 609 North Paca St., Baltimore, MD 21201; (301) 523-3000; Jennifer Glick, Michael Schiaffino, hosts. Three-story 1848 townhouse with enclosed courtyard. Open year-round. Four guest rooms in house; two suites on rear courtyard. Private baths. Rates $45–70 rooms, $95–105 suites; weekly and monthly rates available. Continental breakfast. Children accepted in suites, discouraged in rooms; no pets; Visa/MasterCard/American Express/checks.

DIRECTIONS: take I-95 north to Russell St. exit; stay on Russell which becomes Paca St. Inn is 4 blocks past Lexington Market, across from St. Mary's Seminary.

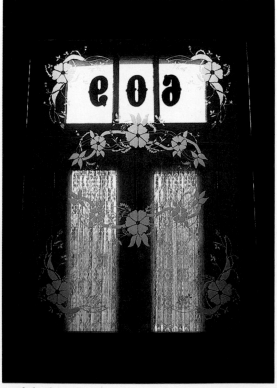

The public sitting room and the front doorway.

ROLAND PARK

A fine collection of Northwest Indian art

A twenty-minute walk from Johns Hopkins University, this solid and elegant home is owned by a professor of medicine at the university, and his wife, a registered nurse with an interest in theater and the arts. While living in the Northwest, they acquired a fine collection of Northwest Indian art, which is displayed throughout the house. The impeccably clean guest room contains such amenities as a rocking chair, desk, attached bath, and a full dressing mirror.

ROLAND PARK. Colonial house with Federal embellishments. Open year-round. One guest room, private bath. Rates $45 single, $60 double. Full breakfast available. No smoking. Twenty-minute walk to Johns Hopkins University. *Represented by The Bed & Breakfast League, Ltd., Washington, DC.*

Entrance hall, showing an English brass rubbing on the landing.

BOLTON HILL

Light-filled guest rooms

Bolton Hill is a gracious urban neighborhood comprised of age-softened brick townhouses and tall shade trees. Just ten blocks from the Inner Harbor and close to Meyerhoff Symphony Hall, Lyric Theater, and the Baltimore Opera, this four-story rowhouse reflects the quiet good taste of its owner. Light-filled guest rooms on the top floor are spacious and comfortable. Guests may use the deck and private courtyard at the rear of the house.

BOLTON HILL. Four-story, turn-of-the-century townhouse. Open year-round. Two guest rooms, shared bath. Rates $45 single, $60 double. Hearty continental breakfast. No pets. On Bolton Hill, within walking district of Meyerhoff Symphony Hall and Lyric Theater. *Represented by The Bed & Breakfast League Ltd., Washington, DC; Sharp and Adams, Baltimore, MD.*

WASHINGTON, D.C.

Built to inspire pride and patriotism

The original plan for the city of Washington was designed by a young French military engineer named Pierre-Charles L'Enfant. Nourished by the splendor of Paris and Versailles, L'Enfant envisioned their grandeur and style transplanted to the New World. Unfortunately, L'Enfant was dismissed before he could execute the plan, and as a result his original design was produced in modified form.

The pattern for Washington is loosely based on L'Enfant's concept of avenues. Named for states, these broad thoroughfares tend to radiate diagonally from the White House, the Mall, and the Capitol Building and are beaded with circles and squares, each ornamented with statuary or trees. These avenues are fixed by a gridwork of streets bearing letter names to the north and south, and numbers to the east and west. Finally,

the city is divided into quadrants, designated NW, NE, SW, and SE.

Though the master plan went somewhat awry—resulting in a complicated tangle of traffic during rush hours—Washington and its monuments are simply grand. Its many symbols of state, including the symmetry, charm, and modesty of the White House, the massive domination of the Capitol Building, and the elegance of the Lincoln and Jefferson memorials, inspire pride and patriotism.

Washington also has more fine museums than any other city in America. It is a pleasure to bask in the presence of American genius, on display at the Corcoran Gallery of Art, or to observe the beautiful architecture of both the East and West Buildings of the National Gallery of Art as they vie with the interior exhibitions. Most people have heard of the Smithsonian Institution, but few realize that it is a family of seven complete and individual museums, which include, among others, the Arts and Industry Building, the National Air and Space Museum, the Hirshhorn Museum and Sculpture Garden, the Freer Gallery of Art, and the Renwick Gallery.

Left, the Lincoln Memorial. Above, 1930s vintage planes in the Smithsonian's Air and Space Museum.

Left and above, a collector's blend of Oriental art and French furniture.

DUPONT CIRCLE

A home becomes a work of art

Only one-half block from the famous Phillips Collection and one block from the DuPont Circle Metro, this spacious townhouse, furnished with an eclectic mix of fine Chinese, Middle Eastern, and European *objects d'art*, is a fascinating study in itself. Having pursued the arts all of her life, the hostess specializes in creating bejeweled icons, a selection of which adorns the staircase wall leading to the second-floor guest rooms. Each bedroom has a warm personality and is equipped with refrigerator, television, and even a buzzer for ordering breakfast. This meal is another work of art. Two house specialties, a carmelized French toast and savory chicken-liver omelet, are worth a special trip. The neighborhood's tree-lined streets are filled with pubs, cafés, bookstores, and specialty shops.

DUPONT CIRCLE. Century-old townhouse with lovely décor. Open year-round. Two guest rooms on second floor and, upon occasion, 2-room suite available in basement. Rates: $40 single, $55 double. Full breakfast. Children in basement suite only; no pets. In DuPont Circle area, near park and within walking distance of Georgetown. *Represented by Sweet Dreams & Toast, Inc., Washington, D.C.*

Bed and breakfast service *par excellence*

Close to the Smithsonian Institution, the Capitol Building, and the famous monuments and government buildings, this townhouse is the home of a professional management consultant, who operates a catering service and who lived in Alaska for thirteen years. She loves to entertain, and her guests are the lucky beneficiaries of that talent. Besides making people comfortable, she also proficiently guides visitors through the ins-and-outs of Washington.

CAPITOL HILL. 1891 townhouse with stunning architectural details, private backyard and patio. Open year-round. Rates $35 single, $50 double. From one to three guest rooms, depending on family then at home; shared bath. Continental breakfast. Inquire about pets. In Capitol Hill neighborhood, close to all government centers, monuments, and the Smithsonian Institution. *Represented by Sweet Dreams & Toast, Inc., Washington, DC.*

Formal dining room set for breakfast, above. Flanking the fireplace, right, is part of the Lladro figurine collection.

Staircase leading to the guest rooms.

Antiques-filled modern townhouse

The owners of this splendid contemporary townhouse make guests feel as if they are in their own home. During the week, visitors may prepare their own breakfast, if they wish, and afterwards sun themselves on the private patio or bicycle through the adjoining park. The displays of Spanish art and a magnificent collection of Lladro figurines are complemented by fine antique furnishings.

CHEVY CHASE. Spacious, English-style townhouse in townhouse community. Open year-round. Rates: $40 single, $55 double. Full breakfast, prepared by guests during the week. Well-behaved pets only. In Chevy Chase, Maryland; all of Washington is accessible by car. *Represented by Sweet Dreams & Toast, Inc., Washington, DC.*

BED & BREAKFAST
IN THE COUNTRY

MAINE

CLEFTSTONE MANOR

Preserves the mood of Victorian gentility

James Blair built his summer home, a modest thirty-three room cottage, high on a rocky ledge overlooking the beautiful isle of Bar Harbor. His winter home in Washington, D.C., later used as an alternate presidential residence known as Blair House, sat across from the White House. Today both homes welcome travelers, Blair House serving as a home to dignitaries visiting the United States. Cleftstone Manor, under the thoughtful ownership of Phyllis and Donald Jackson, is a supremely lovely bed and breakfast inn.

The entire house is furnished with fine antiques, including such unusual pieces as Joseph Pulitzer's awesome writing table. This grand table amply fills the formal dining room and is put to use each day when it is laden with scones and shortbread at tea time and with cheeses and wine in the evening. Breakfast is served on the enclosed sunporch, a light-washed room complemented by white wicker furniture, a collection of Delft china, and masses of greenery.

The bedrooms, each different, are decorated with a confident and sophisticated touch. A favorite for honeymooners is the spacious Romeo and Juliet Room. One corner is given over to a brass canopied bed, draped in white lace. A comfortable love seat faces a working fireplace and the beautifully detailed coffered ceiling deepens the prevailing sense of privacy and luxury. The Glastonbury Room, with high-back Victorian bedstead, red velvet chair, hand-crocheted bedspread, and many decorative grace notes is serene.

CLEFTSTONE MANOR, Eden St., Bar Harbor, ME 04609; (207) 288-4951; Phyllis and Donald Jackson and family, hosts. Open May 15 to Oct. 15. Eighteen double rooms, four with fireplaces, one with balcony; two family suites; mostly private baths. Rates: $32 to $50 double, shared baths, $62 to $85, private baths; rates include breakfast with emphasis on home baking. Four-o'clock tea daily; evening wine and cheese. Numerous restaurants nearby. Children welcome; no pets; Visa/MasterCard/American Express. Owner's son operates hot-air ballooning business at inn.

DIRECTIONS: from points south, take Rte. 1 north to Ellsworth, then follow Rte. 3 into Bar Harbor. Inn is 500 feet past Bluenose Ferry terminal.

Left, the Romeo and Juliet honeymoon suite. Above, Joseph Pulitzer's writing table in the formal dining room.

BLACK FRIAR INN

A lifelong interest in "railroadiana"

Fred Pooler is Bar Harbor's maverick, an energetic entrepeneur who operates a successful restaurant, The Brick Oven; owns the Bar Harbor Trolley Car Company, which runs tours in Fred's private trolley car; and operates a comfortable and casual bed and breakfast.

His "dream come to life," the inn combines many found objects: wood from the junkyard panels bathrooms and the common room ceiling; decorative pressed tin, wooden pillars, and ornate window frames culled from buildings long decayed find new life in common rooms and bedchambers. The common room on the first floor is a cheery combination of wicker, cushions, and plants. Bedrooms feel old-fashioned, mixing antique bed frames and chests against backgrounds of floral wallpapers.

In the morning guests wander into the spotless kitchen, copper work counters gleaming, the aroma of brewed coffee permeating the air. Here you'll see what's cooking and indicate your preference.

BLACK FRIAR INN, 10 Summer St., Bar Harbor, ME 04609; (207) 288-5091; Fred Pooler, host. Comfortable, eclectic shingled house reflects owner's lifelong interest in "railroadiana." Open Memorial Day to Oct. 20. Six guest rooms, each with sink, share four showers. Rates $30 to $50 double, in season; $27 to $45 off season, including full breakfast. Wide selection of dining nearby, including host's own Brick Oven. No children; no pets; major credit cards.

DIRECTIONS: from south, take Rte. 1 to Rte. 3 at Ellsworth. Follow Rte. 3 into Bar Harbor, turn left at sign for downtown district (College St.). Inn is kitty-corner behind the Municipal Bldg. Enter through Municipal Bldg. parking lot.

Innkeeper Fred Pooler is a train buff.

The Siamese shares the house with a Himalyan and a Maine coon cat.

GRANE'S FAIRHAVEN INN

In a charming seaside village

Grane's Fairhaven Inn sits on the banks of the Kennebec and is blessed with acres of softly rolling meadows edged by thick stands of trees. The inn is a rambling grey-shingle cottage decorated in a comfortable and simple style. Amiable innkeepers Gretchen Williams and Jane Wyllie receive accolades for their thoughtfully prepared and presented breakfast. Jane, a dynamo in the kitchen, concocts a wide range of foods for the morning repast. A menu might include homemade scrapple or sausage; finnan haddie; savory soufflés; eggs bronco or Swiss eggs; pancakes embellished with pecans, bananas, cinnamon apples, or Maine blueberries; orange French toast; fresh fruit; and a variety of cereals.

GRANE'S FAIRHAVEN INN, Bath, ME 04530; (207) 443-4391; Gretchen Williams and Jane Wyllie, hostesses. Open all year. Nine guest rooms, most sharing baths. Rates $22 to $30 single, $30 to $50 double. Extra charge for breakfast. Children welcome; advance notice required for pets; smoking restricted; no credit cards.

DIRECTIONS: follow Rte. 1 north through Brunswick to West Bath/New Meadows exit. At top of exit ramp turn right; at first stop sign turn right and then first immediate left (visible from stop sign). Drive 7/10 mile and take a sharp right. Drive 8/10 mile and turn left. Inn is ½ mile up the hill.

ENGLISH MEADOWS INN

Like a visit to Grandma's

Gene Kelly bought Gussie English's country boarding house with a mind to renting out a room or two for a little extra income. Never in his wildest dreams did he imagine the devoted following that English Meadows Inn would inspire.

The inn sits on rolling and wooded acreage that still feels like country, though today the property dovetails with Kennebunkport's commercial center. Century-old lilacs, which perform gorgeously and fragrantly each spring, provide a curtain of privacy for the inn. Rooms in the main house are filled with antiques, rag and hooked rugs, and beautiful old patchwork quilts. Additional guest quarters in the adjoining rustic barn combine knotty pine, an open fireplace, wicker furniture, and views of field and garden to create a comfortable camplike atmosphere.

Breakfast prepared by Claudia is ample and delicious. One guest was so enamored of her sour dough French toast and maple syrup that he changed clothes, donned dark glasses, and seated himself for a second round. The poor fellow was found out, but the compliment was appreciated nonetheless.

Buttons, the inn's shaggy top dog, completes the scene and occasionally upstages Gene and Claudia, whose mutual senses of humor defy succinct description. Suffice it to say, Archie Bunker could take lessons from Gene.

ENGLISH MEADOWS INN, R.F.D. #1, Rte. 35, Kennebunkport, ME 04046; (207) 967-5766; Gene Kelly and Claudia Kelly Butler, hosts. A stay at this *circa* 1860 Victorian farmhouse is like a visit to Grandma's. Open April 1 through October. Fourteen guest rooms with semi-private baths; two apartments. Rates: $28 to $30 single, $50 to $60 double, varying seasonally; apartments $375 to $450 per week, monthly rates available; rates include "famous" breakfast. Excellent dining nearby, especially seafood. No children under twelve; no pets; no credit cards. Maine coast is vacationer's dream for recreation, scenery, historic sites.

DIRECTIONS: take Maine Turnpike to exit 3 (Kennebunk). Turn left on Rte. 35 south. Inn is five miles ahead on right.

Guests like to make themselves at home in the living room.

Left, China and glass beautifully displayed. Above, a spacious third-floor guest room.

CAPTAIN JEFFERDS INN

A New England sea captain's house

The Kennebunkport historic district is peppered with gracious "cottages" built in the early 1800s by seafaring captains who traveled the globe in pursuit of treasure.

Warren Fitzsimmons and Don Kelly were partners in a successful antiques business when they bought one of these—Captain Jefferds' home—and brought the place to vibrant life. If, upon entering, you have a sense of déjà vu, don't doubt your feelings. The work of these two gifted innkeepers has been featured on the covers of several prestigious home decorating magazines. Two cobalt blue vases displaying a bounty of brilliant silk flowers flank the formal entryway. To the left is the breakfast room where guests gather each morning to be served by Don, dressed in butler's whites. Warren mans the kitchen, serving up custardy French toast, delicate pancakes, and perfectly turned eggs.

Each bedroom is special. Several are decorated in Laura Ashley's simple prints; others are dressed in muted tones that dramatize an elegant chaise, bird's-eye maple chest, or Chinese screen.

The collection of antiques in this inn is endlessly fascinating. Warren and Don buy only the truest examples of a representative period—there are no reproductions in the entire inn—and the place practically vibrates from the beauty produced by their combined collections. Though Warren and Don were personally attracted to American antiques, from tramp and shell art to twig furniture and Indian baskets, the inn's formal lines required sterling silver and crystal as well. It all works.

THE CAPTAIN JEFFERDS INN, Pearl St., Box 691, Kennebunkport, ME 04046; (207) 967-2311; Don Kelly and Warren Fitzsimmons, hosts. 1804 Federal style sea captain's house. Open all year except Christmas Eve and Day, with weekday closings during winter months. Eleven guest rooms in main house, mostly private baths; three efficiency apartments in carriage house. Rates $45 single, $60 to $73 double; apartments $475 to $750 per week, in season; guests in main house are treated to full breakfast, with seasonal specialties. No children under twelve; pets welcome, with advance notice; smoking restricted; no credit cards.

DIRECTIONS: take Maine Turnpike to exit 3 to Rte. 35. Follow signs through Kennebunk to Kennebunkport. Turn left at traffic light and cross drawbridge. Turn right at monument onto Ocean Ave. Proceed ³⁄₁₀ mile to Arundel Wharf and turn left onto Pearl St.

NEW HAMPSHIRE

THE INN AT CHRISTIAN SHORE

Make yourself at home

The Inn at Christian Shore offers visitors to historic Portsmouth an opportunity to relax in one of the city's historic homes and partake of one of the grandest breakfasts anywhere.

After applying considerable energy and talent to the restoration of this sea captain's home, Louis Sochia, Thomas Towey, and Charles Litchfield opened their cozy and comfortable house to the public. The dining room is particularly charming with exposed beams, dark blue wainscoting, open fireplace, harvest table and Hitchcock chairs, and attractively displayed antique prints and primitive paintings.

Breakfast begins with juice or fresh fruit in season and a warm fruit loaf, possibly Tom's special banana-blueberry bread. Next, guests are served an egg dish and steak, pork tenderloin, or ham fried with pineapple. This substantial "main course" is always accompanied by home-fried potatoes and a vegetable in season—broccoli, cauliflower, or possibly steamed squash—a slice of tomato on a bed of lettuce, toast, and a hot beverage.

Though after such bounteous fare, food is not foremost in one's mind, Portsmouth offers an amazing array of wonderful restaurants. A short distance from the inn is the renowned Blue Strawberry, which is noted for skillfully prepared dishes created by a chef of rare talent and ingenuity.

THE INN AT CHRISTIAN SHORE, 335 Maplewood Ave., Portsmouth, NH 03801; (603) 431-6770; Charles Litchfield, Thomas Towey, and Louis Sochia, hosts. Sea captain's house, Federal style *circa* 1800. Open all year. Six guest rooms, including one single; private and shared baths. Rates $30 single all year, $35 to $50 double, varying seasonally, includes extravagant breakfast. Wine served in afternoon. Good restaurants within walking distance. Children welcome; pets welcome, with advance notice; Visa/MasterCard.

DIRECTIONS: from Boston, take I-95 to exit 5 and proceed to Portsmouth Rotary Circle. Drive halfway around to Rte. 1, proceeding north to Maplewood Ave. exit (last exit before bridge) and turn right. Inn is sixth house on left.

Host Louis Sochia in the living room.

". . . and the snow lay round about, deep and crisp and even."

HAVERHILL INN

1810 Federal house near village green

In its heyday, Haverhill was a county seat, and prosperity left its mark in the form of grand mansions, many sitting high on the rise overlooking the lovely Connecticut River and Vermont's rolling hills. When the railroad bypassed Haverhill, the town stood still. Today you can't find a grocery, drug store, or even a general store. "Modernization" has never touched this island of beauty, and Haverhill is richer for its loss.

The Haverhill Inn is one of those elegantly proportioned mansions that overlooks the river. It emanates a calm and tranquility that speaks well of its keepers, Katharine DeBoer and Stephen Campbell. But this peaceful atmosphere can also be traced to older inhabitants. Three volumes of data and letters have been compiled on the history of Haverhill and the house. Tracing its lineage,

readers discover that each owner bestowed genuine love on this home. This fortunate history has left its mark.

Today the inn comprises four guest rooms. Each is spacious and each has a working fireplace. The living room, which contains Katharine's baby grand piano, is a comfortable gathering spot, where guests can enjoy a glass of sherry, cup of tea, or a good read. Both Katharine and Stephen pursue careers outside innkeeping. She is a soloist soprano, who gives concerts and teaches. Stephen has a thriving career as a computer programming consultant. Since most of their work is done out of their home, the inn is always well tended.

In summer Katharine plants a large garden from which guests enjoy a bounty of fresh produce. Stephen is a dedicated and gifted cook who makes breakfast a very special event, especially on Sunday.

HAVERHILL INN, Dartmouth College Hwy., Rte. 10, Haverhill, NH 03765; (603) 989-5961; Stephen Campbell and Katharine DeBoer, hosts. French spoken. 1810 Federal style house on quiet street near village green. Open all year. Four guest rooms, all private baths. Rates: $40 single, $50 double, with $10 per additional occupant, including full breakfast, Sunday Special. Afternoon tea and coffee. Restaurants nearby. Older children welcome; pets discouraged; no credit cards.

DIRECTIONS: from Hanover, take Rte. 10 North 27 miles. From NYC (6 hrs.), take I-91 North to exit 15 (Fairlee, Vt.), cross river to Oxford, N.H., and proceed north on Rte. 10. From Boston, I-93 to Plymouth, Rte. 25 west to Haverhill.

BEAL HOUSE INN

Candelit breakfasts

The Beal House Inn feels more like a sociable country inn than does the average bed and breakfast. Doug and Brenda Clickenger operate a warm and cheerful hostelry, one that welcomes guests into comfortable common rooms filled with books and magazines, and bedrooms decorated generously with antiques. The intrinsic charm of The Beal House, besides being a reflection of thoughtful ownership, is due to the fact that the entire inn is an antiques shop. With the exception of a collection of rugs original to the inn and a few select items, everything you look at, sleep atop, sit in, or admire is for sale. What finer way to shop for a bed or chair than to live with it for a time. An antiques shop/inn makes for an ever-changing decor, since a room that loses its elaborate Victorian canopied bed might in turn gain a weighty sleigh bed or a pair of simple pencil post twins.

The Beal House Inn is located at the foot of Littleton's Main Street, where it serves as a graceful transition between shops and residences. An extension of downtown, the inn feels Littleton's pulse, and residents love to visit, especially in the morning when Doug's breakfast is served to guests and public alike. Because it is the only meal they serve, the Clickengers go out of their way to make it a memorable occasion. The dining room is candlelit, and Brenda dresses in old-fashioned garb reminiscent of the mid-1800s, when the inn was a farmhouse on the edge of town. Doug has gained a reputation for both his extra-creamy scrambled eggs, served piping hot in a glass hen, and his towering popovers. Each morning the dining room is the center of activity. This quiet bustle lends to the Beal House the kind of cozy atmosphere that is the hallmark of all successful country inns.

THE BEAL HOUSE INN, Main St., Littleton, NH 03561; (603) 444-2661; Clickenger family, hosts. Spanish spoken by daughter. Frame Federal-style house has been inn-*cum*-antiques-shop for over 50 years. Open all year. Fifteen guest rooms, ten with private baths. Rates $25 to $70, according to season and amenities. Additional charge for full country breakfast served tavern-style. Evening tea and snacks. Current menus and reservation service for local dining. Children welcome; pet boarding nearby; smoking restricted; major credit cards.

DIRECTIONS: from I-93, take exit 41 into Littleton. Turn left onto Main St. to inn, at junction of Rtes. 18 and 302.

Left, the staircase leading to the guest rooms is bedecked with whimsical bookends and doorstops.

VERMONT

MIDDLETOWN SPRINGS INN

An incredible collection of dolls

Jean Hendrickson's grandmother started the whole thing when she bought that first doll. Jean's mother followed in her mother's footsteps. By the time Jean inherited a two-generation collection of dolls to add to her own, she had quite a gallery. Mel Hendrickson, a slim version of Kris Kringle complete with twinkle, estimates that the doll population at Middletown Springs Inn numbers around three thousand, and Jean explains that the appeal of this collection lies in its variety.

At first glance the Hendrickson's first floor looks like an orderly version of Dicken's Old Curiosity Shop, with dolls filling cabinet after cabinet.

There are so many interesting details to absorb that a person could spend a very satisfying weekend without ever leaving the house. Lunch is certainly an unnecessary excursion after one of Mel's breakfasts. A wonderful cook and bread baker, Mel serves up delicate silver dollar blueberry pancakes with Vermont maple syrup and sausage, eggs Priscilla, bananas Foster, spiced hamballs, his very own sticky buns, and the Mel McMuffin.

Bedrooms are furnished with antiques, and each is well-stocked with light reading material for night owls and early risers. Plush bathrobes are provided for those rooms whose bathroom is a few steps down the hall.

THE MIDDLETOWN SPRINGS INN, Middletown Springs, VT 05757; (802) 235-2198; Jean and Mel Hendrickson, hosts. Seven guest rooms in house, three guest rooms in barn. Shared and private baths. Open year-round. Rates: $50 single; $65 double; $30 third person. Full, hearty breakfast; *prix fixe* dinner by prior arrangement. Children discouraged; no pets; Visa/MasterCard/checks.

DIRECTIONS: from New York City, take Taconic Pkwy. north to Rte. 23 east to Great Barrington, Mass. (Rte. 7). Take 7 north to Manchester, Vt., to Rte. 30 north. Take 30 to Pawlet to Rte. 133 north, which takes you to Middletown Springs. Inn is on village green.

Left, Jean and Mel Hendrickson and friend.

SHOREHAM INN AND COUNTRY STORE

A tiny town on Lake Champlain

Surrounded by apple orchards and dairy farms, and bordered on one side by Lake Champlain's sinuous tail, the Shoreham Inn and its adjoining Country Store form the heart of tiny Shoreham, Vermont. The inn's atmosphere, reflecting its beautiful setting and kind proprietors, is warm, gentle, and welcoming.

Built in 1799 as a public house, it allows today's inngoers to walk the same wooden floorboards that its first visitors trod. These wide planks are partially hidden by lustrous old area rugs and an irregular collection of antiques—none matches, but all work together—that please the eye and comfort the spirit.

Cleo and Fred Alter love original art, a taste fully developed during the days they worked together in printing and graphic design, and they exercise this love by showing the work of gifted local artists. Not a gallery per se, the inn doesn't sell work but the Alters do take pleasure in sharing beautiful things with others.

Breakfast is low-keyed. On each table guests find a canning jar filled with granola, pitchers of milk and juice, local honey and preserves, muffins or scones, and cheese. Since this is apple country, Cleo always serves the fruit in one form or another. Glass cookie jars in the center of each large dining table are always stocked with homebaked sweets for snackers.

The Country Store, just next to the inn, supplies everything from magazines and groceries to hardware and wine. The Alters operate a small delicatessen in back, where you can order a pizza or sandwiches and salads. Picnic tables on the village green beckon on a summer day.

SHOREHAM INN AND COUNTRY STORE, Shoreham, VT 05770; (802) 897-5081; Cleo and Fred Alter, hosts. Built as an inn in 1799, the Shoreham served as a way station for floating railroad bridge and ferry across Lake Champlain. Open all year. Nine guest rooms, some accommodating four people, shared baths. Rates $30 single, $50 double, including light breakfast. Numerous restaurants in area. Children welcome; no pets; no credit cards. Area offers aquatic and other sports, museums, Ft. Ticonderoga, Morgan horse farm.

DIRECTIONS: inn is 12 miles southwest of Middlebury. Follow Rte. 22A from Fairhaven to Rte. 74 west. From Burlington, take 7 south to 22A at Vergennes, then take 74 west into Shoreham. Ticonderoga ferry operates to and from Shoreham.

MAPLE CREST FARM

Ancestral home and working dairy farm

Maple Crest Farm has been in the same family for five generations, ever since it opened its doors as Gleason Tavern in 1808. The resulting atmosphere is multi-layered and rich. This is not a manicured vacation resort; rather it is a working dairy farm with a hundred head of cattle.

The dairy barns.

The architectural styles in the farmhouse are interesting. Gleason built a colonial structure with Federal embellishments. Enter the Victorian age with its mandatory decorative porches and ornate hearth treatments. And finally the twentieth century brought with it inelegant linoleum and acoustical tiles. Though each age will still be represented, Donna Smith, Maple Crest's gracious hostess, is slowly but surely removing the more offensive "improvements" and uncovering original floors and beams.

Guests spend hours poring over diaries and the family bible, observing a dairy farm at work, and in the spring participating in maple-sugaring.

Acres of hiking paths become excellent cross-country ski trails when snow cooperates. All in all, Maple Crest Farm is a diamond in the rough and well worth a visit.

MAPLE CREST FARM, Box 120, Cuttingsville, VT 05738; (802) 492-3367; William and Donna Smith, hosts. Closed first two weeks of November, Thanksgiving, Christmas Eve and Day. Four guest rooms with shared bath, one two-bedroom apartment. Rates: $28 double; breakfast included first and last morning of stay. Restaurants in nearby Rutland. No preschool children; no pets; no credit cards.

DIRECTIONS: from Manchester, take Rte. 7 north to Rte. 103 (just south of Rutland). Turn right on 103, cross railroad tracks, and drive up the hill. Watch for "Meadow Sweet Herb Farm" sign. At hilltop, bear left on Lincoln Hill Rd. and continue 2 miles; farm is in Shrewesbury on right, across from church and meeting hall.

Donna's breakfast bread.

1811 HOUSE

A classic inn; a classic village

This is not just another inn. The groomed and elegant 1811 House is impeccable inside and out. When Mary and Jack Hirst found this historic building, ideally situated next to the classic New England spired church on the equally classic Manchester village green, it was in need of complete renovation. They began by removing aluminum siding that encased the structure and hiring eight men to remove two centuries of paint. It took workers ten full weeks to uncover the original wood. Then the Federal capitals and moldings began to fall apart. So the Hirsts copied all of the embellishments and reinstated identical decorative moldings. Finally, the "two-over-two" Victorian cylinder glass windows were replaced by colonial-style twelve-pane glass. Jack didn't rest until each pane was filled with irregular antique glass.

The Hirsts tackled the interior with the same dedication and energy, painstakingly restoring original detail and adding private baths for each

A second floor guest room.
Another view of the inn can seen on page 2,
facing the title page.

An unusual French fashion plate.

of the ten bedrooms. In the center of the building they created an English pub, in honor of Mary's homeland, complete with dartboard and working fireplace.

All of the rooms in the house are simple and lovely. The first-floor parlors and dining room are furnished from Mary's collection of fine English antiques, crystal, and paintings of country scenes. Each bedroom has its own color scheme and personality.

Britain inspires American inns, and Mary's authentic English breakfast shows us one reason why. Guests might be treated to kippers, sautéed chicken livers, or sole meunière; grilled tomatoes; sautéed apples and mushrooms, in addition to eggs, bacon, fried bread, and fresh-squeezed orange juice, all served on fine china and crystal.

1811 HOUSE, Manchester Village, VT 05254; (802) 362-1811; Mary and Jack Hirst, hosts. Excellent example of Federal architecture, which was long a famous summer resort in the 1800s. Open year-round. Ten guest rooms, private baths. Rates: $75 to $100 double. Full English-style breakfast. No children under sixteen; no pets; major credit cards. Excellent dining in the area and occasional dinners served on premises for guests. Hiking, fishing, tennis, golf, swimming, antiquing, winter skiing.

DIRECTIONS: from Bennington, Vt., drive north on historic Rte. 7A. Inn is in Manchester Village on the green, next to the Congregational Church (with spire).

Marlboro is the classic New England village, consisting of a church, a post office, and an inn.

WHETSTONE INN

"The nicest inn in New England"

Jean and Harry Boardman moved to southern Vermont from southern California where Harry was secretary general for the Council for Biology and Human Affairs at the Salk Institute and where Jean edited a linguistics journal. Over the years Harry had stayed at this historic inn while in the area to give seminars on humanist subjects. And though neither he nor Jean had ever given thought to becoming innkeepers, six months after discovering that this 1786 tavern was for sale, the Boardmans were running the Whetstone Inn.

Warmhearted, intellectually stimulating, and decorated in a no-frills, comfortable style, the Whetstone elicits spontaneous testimonials. Rosy-cheeked from an afternoon of cross-country skiing, one thoroughly satisfied guest burst forth with unrestrained enthusiasm: "Do you want to know about this place? It's the epitome, the absolutely nicest inn in New England. Harry and Jean make it what it is. Jean is just the best chef. You can't believe what her cooking is like. . ."

Jean's cooking is, indeed, renowned, from her masterful handling of breakfast foods to the dinners she creates several times a week. Fortunate patrons might dine on homemade soup; leg of lamb with plum sauce; filet of beef or veal with white wine sauce; fresh salad; and, for dessert, a pie shell filled with chocolate mousse, or, the all-time favorite, apple cheddar cheese pie.

Tiny Marlboro is a classic, picture postcard village as well as a year-round resort. Summer brings many joys including the seven-week Marlboro Music Festival, a feast of chamber music with Rudolph Serkin as artistic director. Luminaries from the world of music, from Avery Fisher to Jean Pierre Rampal, might be table partners at one of Jean's dinners. Fall color is brilliant, and the loveliness of the flowers and vivid greens of spring beggars description. During the winter season the Whetstone offers excellent cross-country skiing on its eleven acres of hills and meadows, while downhill skiing is found a short drive away.

A "pre-Murphy" bed.

Left, heading for the cross-country ski trails.

WHETSTONE INN, Marlboro, VT 05344; (802) 254-2500; Jean and Harry Boardman, Hosts. French and some German spoken. Post-and-beam construction inn, built as a tavern around 1786. Open year-round. Thirteen guest rooms, some with kitchenettes, some that accommodate four; shared and private baths. Rates: $20 singles, $35 to $55 doubles; $2 infant, $6 child, $10 third adult (15 and above). Hearty breakfast served; variety of good restaurants in area. Pets discouraged; checks accepted; Downhill and cross-country skiing, hiking, Marlboro Music Festival.
DIRECTIONS: drive 8 miles west from Brattleboro, Vt., on Rte. 9. Marlboro is ¼ mile off Rte. 9.

MASSACHUSETTS

NORTHFIELD COUNTRY HOUSE

A well-kept secret revealed

Hidden in the hills of the beautiful Connecticut River Valley, Northfield Country House is one of those special places that visitors hope to keep a secret, all to themselves.

The aura of romance begins as you wind your way up the drive. Trees suddenly part to reveal a gracefully proportioned English manor house built in 1901 by a wealthy Boston shipbuilder who had an eye for beauty and the purse to pursue it. He insisted upon the finest handcarved cherry wainscoting, mantels, and doors; a broad staircase; leaded glass windows; and a twelve-foot stone hearth in which is embedded the message, "Love Warms The Heart As Fire The Hearth."

Janice Gamache has decorated her country house with a wonderful sense of color and design. The living room invites conversation or reading, its three plush and generous couches framing the stone hearth. Janice's desire was to recreate in each bedroom all the comforts of home but to make each room "a little more special." A crimson hideaway with working fireplace, velvet settee, and thick comforter on an antique bed feels rich and warm; another blue and white chamber complete with brass and iron bedstead and white wicker armchair is crisp, fresh, and old-fashioned. Janice pays attention to extras: lovely linens, antique lace pillows, and charming bits of china.

Breakfast, which is served on the porch in the summer and in the cherry-paneled dining room when the weather is wet or cold, is simply splendid, as are the *prix fixe* dinners offered several times a week.

NORTHFIELD COUNTRY HOUSE, School St., Northfield, MA 03160; (413) 498-2692; Janice and Paul Gamache, hosts. Spanish spoken by Paul. English manor house set on 16 acres. Open year-round. Seven guest rooms, shared baths. Rates: $30 to $60. Full breakfast served daily, five-course dinner served Thurs.-Sat. Checks accepted.

DIRECTIONS: take I-91 to Exit 28A. Follow Rte. 10 north to Northfield Center. School St. is in center of town, at the firehouse. Turn at firehouse and drive 9/10 of a mile. Inn driveway is on right. *Note:* Since street becomes narrow dirt road, driving in snowy or wet conditions can be difficult. Please have good tires!

Left, the dining room set for breakfast, with Janice's delicious Swiss cereal. Above, each guest room has its own character.

Hosts Brad Wagstaff and Leslie Miller.

THE OLD INN ON THE GREEN

A sleepy village floodlit at night

Brad Wagstaff bought this charming eighteenth-century inn as a restoration project a half-dozen years ago. Leslie Miller came to the Berkshires to train as a baker, rented a room in the partially renovated inn, and fell in love with Brad and the Berkshires.

The New Marlborough green is pastoral and idyllic, a sleepy village whose cluster of Greek Revival relics—most especially the Town Meeting House, dramatically floodlit at night—reflects a burst of commerce long since past. A short walk along the town's quiet main road takes strollers past Brad's flock of sheep and large herd of dairy cattle. Wander down the lane just next to the inn to discover some of the most spectacular scenery in the Berkshire Mountains.

The inn, which is being meticulously restored to its original glory, is casual and wonderfully atmospheric. Bedrooms are furnished with a combination of classic antiques and funky art deco and forties accoutrements. The second-floor balcony was made for a leisurely morning of reading, coffee drinking, or just watching the sun move higher in the sky.

The inn features a formal dinner each Saturday night, served in the three downstairs dining rooms. With the aid of a talented local chef, Leslie and Brad offer a five-course *prix fixe* menu that changes with the seasons and unfolds beautifully in the soft glow of candlelight and firelight.

THE OLD INN ON THE GREEN, New Marlborough, MA 01230; (413) 229-7924; Leslie Miller and Brad Wagstaff, hosts. Spanish spoken by Leslie. Built in 1760 as an inn, this Greek Revival gem also once served as tavern, stagecoach stop, general store, and post office. Open weekends year-round. Four guest rooms; shared baths. Rates: $50 per room. Continental breakfast. No pets; checks accepted; no credit cards. Summer theater nearby; excellent dining in area.

DIRECTIONS: from New York City, take Taconic Pkwy. to Rte. 23 exit. Take 23 through Great Barrington and go east toward Monterrey. Turn right on Rte. 57 before Monterry and follow for 5.7 miles. From Boston, take Mass. Tnpke. to Lee exit. Take Rte. 7 through Stockbridge to Rte. 23, and 23 toward Monterrey, following directions above.

WALKER HOUSE INN

For music buffs

In California Peggy and Richard Houdek both pursued careers in the arts. Peggy, a trained opera singer, was managing editor of *Performing Arts* magazine. Richard was contributing music critic to the *Los Angeles Times* and president of Guild Opera of Los Angeles. In Lenox, summer home of the Boston Symphony Orchestra, the Houdeks feel at home running the Walker House, which attracts performers in the arts.

Each large room in the Federal-style, eighteen-room mansion is named after a famous composer and decorated accordingly. The Puccini guest room is emotional and robust, with romantic rose-colored walls, a brass bed, and a portrait of the composer. Chopin is a delicate blend of pinks, blues and lavender; Beethoven displays strong and masculine wallpaper that sets off a bust of the composer.

WALKER HOUSE INN, 74 Walker, St., Lenox, MA 02140; (413) 637-1271; Peggy and Richard Houdek, hosts. Spanish and French spoken and operatic German and Italian. Open year-round, nine rooms with private baths. Rates fluctuate from $40 to $105 with seasons and accommodations. Continental breakfast, afternoon tea. No children under eight; pets by prior arrangement; checks accepted.

DIRECTIONS: from New York City, take Taconic Pkwy. to Rte. 23 exit and continue on 23 east to Great Barrington. Take Rte. 7 to 7A (Lenox Centre) and turn left. Inn is first building on left after stop sign.

Peggy and Richard Houdek.

MERRELL TAVERN INN

Fine antiques in a stagecoach inn

Catering to travelers since the 1800s, the old Merrell Tavern has been painstakingly restored to its former glory by Charles and Faith Reynolds. It is now elegantly furnished with fine Sheraton and Heppelwhite antiques the Reynolds have collected over twenty-five years. Canopied, four-poster, and pencil-post bedsteads with deluxe mattresses, sought out for their exquisite comfort, ensure a pleasurable night's sleep. In the morning guests gather in the tavern for breakfast, which may feature Charles' special omelets, pancakes, and sausages, or perhaps a new find from a cookbook. A visit will reveal more treasures; there is not space here to do them justice.

MERRELL TAVERN INN, Rte. 102, South Lee., MA 01260; (413) 243-1794; Charles and Faith Reynolds, hosts. Closed Christmas Eve and Day. Seven guest rooms in inn proper, one in old summer kitchen, one in old smokehouse; fireplaces in three rooms, private and shared baths. Rates: $40 to $95 double, according to season and amenities, weekend packages available. All rates include full breakfast. No pets; major credit cards.

DIRECTIONS: exit Mass. Turnpike at Lee (exit 2) and follow Rte. 102 three miles toward Stockbridge.

THE INN AT STOCKBRIDGE

Ultimate breakfasts by a professional

"My fixation on buildings that would make good inns became the family joke," laughs Lee Weitz from the comfort of a chintz-covered couch in her book-lined living room. Lee has realized her dream in The Inn at Stockbridge, which combines the graciousness of a 1906 pillared "summer house" with the formality of sweeping porticos and fanlight windows. Seasoned inngoers, Lee and Don Weitz have included all the special touches they most enjoy at their favorite inns.

A home economist by profession, Lee ran a test kitchen in New Jersey in which she developed and tested recipes. With solid years of experience and equal emphasis on presentation and good taste, Lee creates a breakfast that is a delight. Served on Spode, Wedgewood, or other fine china, specialties include savory soufflés, eggs Benedict accompanied by a champagne cocktail, thick-sliced French toast garnished with orange-apricot-Grand Marnier whipped butter, and homemade coffee cakes and muffins.

During the summer the swimming pool and twelve acres of yard crisscrossed with walking and jogging trails offer relaxation and solitude. In the winter these same trails are groomed for cross-country skiing. To avoid dinner-hour crowds, you might request one of Lee's fabulous custom dinners, prepared on advance notice.

THE INN AT STOCKBRIDGE, Box 2033, Rte. 7, Stockbridge, MA 01262; (413) 298-3337; Lee and Don Weitz, hosts. Some German spoken. Seven guest rooms, two with shared baths. Open year-round. Rates for double occupancy: $60–130, July, Aug., Oct.; $50–95, rest of year; $20 for 3rd person. Full breakfast. No children under eight; no pets; credit cards accepted.

DIRECTIONS: from New York City, take Taconic Pkwy. to Rte. 23 exit. Take 23 through Great Barrington to Rte. 7 and 7 through Stockbridge. Inn is 1 mile north of Stockbridge, just north of Mass. Tnpke. underpass. From eastern Mass., take Mass. Tnpke. to Lee exit and rd. to Stockbridge.

One of the two living rooms dressed up for Christmas.

CORNELL HOUSE

Cabaret music still echoes here

Cornell House, owned and operated by Chuck Bowers, is a comfortable mix of antiques, period pieces, and humorous high camp. In the main foyer the stern countenance of great-great grandmother Charity Cornell, for whom the house is named, observes all comings and goings—and whatever the goings-on, she does not approve! Nearby, Chuck's "disaster corner," made up of framed front pages of newspapers, commemorates great catastrophes of the last century.

Facing the four-hundred-acre Kennedy Park, open to the public year-round, the communal breakfast parlor with floor-to-ceiling windows is a favorite gathering spot. In the evening, dining tables transform into game tables and conversation goes on into the wee hours. A speakeasy during Prohibition, this graceful Queen Anne Victorian still echoes with cabaret music. Chuck's love of music is great, and his music room, dominated by a beautiful baby grand piano, reflects this feeling; its walls are filled with colorful sheet music framed and neatly hung.

Behind the main house is Hill House, a two-story converted barn, especially charming in warm months when shuttered windows are accented with flowering window boxes. Decorated with an assortment of undistinguished but comfortable furniture, the atmosphere is warm and cheering.

Perhaps the best reason to stay at Cornell House, besides its desirable location central to both busy Lenox Center and Tanglewood, is the very reasonable tariff, which remains so even in the height of the season.

CORNELL HOUSE, 197 Pittsfield Rd., Lenox, MA 01240; (413) 637-0562; Chuck Bowers, host. Charming inn, *circa* 1888, invites rumination and repose, Victorian-style. Open all year. Four guest rooms in main house, 12 in "Hill House," shared baths. Rates $40 to $55 main house, $30 to $45 Hill House, according to season and amenities; rates include light breakfast. Excellent dining nearby. No children under twelve; no pets; Visa/MasterCard. The Berkshires offer year-round recreation, cultural events, historic sites, antiques.

DIRECTIONS: from NYC, take the Taconic Pkwy. to Rte. 23 exit. Take 23E through Great Barrington to Rte. 7. Take Rte. 7 to Rte. 7A (Lenox Centre) and turn left. Drive through Lenox and up hill to inn on left, just past church. From Mass. Turnpike, take Lee exit 2. Turn right onto Rte. 20W and drive through Lee. Turn left onto Rte. 183 and proceed to Lenox Centre.

Left, a king's ransom in Tin Pan Alley sheet music adorns the walls of the music room.

Breakfast is served in the main living room.

THE TURNING POINT

Once frequented by Daniel Webster

The acquisition of an old stagecoach stop was a turning point for Shirley and Irv Yost. Situated at the turning point in the road, the inn reflects their commitment to a new lifestyle that includes a growing passion for good food.

Breakfast is worth the trip in itself. As Shirley explains, "During college our children changed to vegetarian diets, and this sparked our interest. After several years of experimenting with this diet, one thing led to another, and before we knew it we opened a bed and breakfast devoted to good, delicious food. A friend of ours has suggested that we bill ourselves as *Breakfast and Bed.*"

The focus of each breakfast is whole grains, though the Yosts can cater to wheat-free and other special diets. An average meal might include feather-light whole wheat-and-bran pancakes served with maple syrup, hot baked fruits or fresh fruit salad, eggs, juice, and grain coffee, herbal tea, and the more common brews. Irv often makes a frittata flavored with a mixture of summer vegetables, a robust concoction that he has earlier frozen to provide a cure for the winter blahs. To fill out each abundant meal, Shirley bakes whole grain fruit breads, which she serves with apple butter or natural peanut butter. The Yosts make every effort to offer foods that contain no preservatives or chemicals.

A stay at the Turning Point, which is furnished with an eclectic mix of antiques and well-loved pieces from their home, is casual, comfortable, and very satisfying.

THE TURNING POINT, Rte. 23 and Lake Buel Rd., RD-2 Box 140, Great Barrington, MA 01230; (413) 528-4777; Irv and Shirley Yost, hosts. Federal style older section of house was once tavern-inn frequented by Daniel Webster. Open all year, with occasional off-season closings. Seven guest rooms, most sharing baths. Rates: $35 to $40 single, $50 to $55 double, according to season. Includes elaborate vegetarian breakfast; special diets accommodated. Afternoon tea. Wide range of good dining nearby. Children welcome; no pets; no smoking; no credit cards. Prime Berkshire location offers year-round recreation, sight-seeing, antiquing.

DIRECTIONS: from NYC, take Taconic Pkwy. to Rte. 23. Inn is 21 miles east on Rte. 23 (through Great Barrington) at Lake Buel Rd. From Boston, take Mass. Turnpike to Lee exit (2) onto Rte. 102 W, through Stockbridge to Rte. 750. Follow to Rte. 23, turn left; 2½ miles to inn.

THE COLONEL EBENEZER CRAFTS INN

Owned by the Publick House

Built in 1786 by David Fiske, Esq., The Colonel Ebenezer Crafts Inn is a contemporary of its famous neighbor, Old Sturbridge Village. The inn is well-situated atop Fiske Hill, along a quiet road where peace reigns supreme, and it is blessed with landscaped grounds capacious enough for a large swimming pool, as well as ongoing badminton, croquet, and frisbee tournaments. The house is a large, eight-bedroom colonial-that-grew, filled with a compatible collection of antiques and period reproductions. The living room combines the elegance of a baby grand piano, a massive antique oriental area rug, and formal colonial moldings with the comforts of a television/library alcove and bright, plant-filled sunroom. Each cozy bedroom is stocked with a supply of fresh fruits and cookies, terrycloth robes, extra pillows, and a pot of jam to take home as a memento.

At breakfast, guests fall heir to the bounty of the bakery of the Publick House, Craft's big sister inn, with sinfully delicious, freshly baked pecan sticky buns, spicy pumpkin or blueberry muffins, or old-fashioned cornbread sticks. This meal can be taken in the casual first-floor parlor or from a breakfast tray in bed. For a more substantial meal the Publick House dining room, one mile down the road, offers a classic version of New England red flannel hash, apple pie with cheddar cheese, a variety of egg dishes, and celestial pancakes served with hot maple syrup. Known for its high-quality foods and generous portions, the Publick House is a good choice for afternoon and evening meals as well.

THE COLONEL EBENEZER CRAFTS INN, c/o Publick House, On the Common, Sturbridge, MA 01566; (617) 347-3313; Patricia and Henri Bibeau, hosts. Federal style house open all year. Eight guest rooms, including two suites, all with private baths; rollaways and cribs available. Room rates $65 to $73 double, according to season and amenities; Cottage Suite $90 to $95, varying seasonally; including light breakfast featuring home-baked breads. Excellent dining nearby. Children welcome; no pets; major credit cards. Old Sturbridge Village brings pre-Revolutionary America to life.

DIRECTIONS: from Albany or Boston, take Mass. Turnpike to Exit 9. Bear left (do not go toward Old Sturbridge Village) to Publick House on Rte. 131. Inquire within for directions. From Hartford, take I-84 East, which becomes I-86 and continues to Sturbridge. Take Exit 3. Bear right, then turn left and follow road to back entrance of Publick House. Inquire within for directions to inn.

The building on the right contains a private suite, and the grounds keep the children occupied.

Hostess Marilyn Mudry makes all the quilts.

HAWTHORNE INN

Steeped in American history

Concord, Massachusetts, is among those rare geographical points that seem to emit a force that attracts, inspires, and provokes man to action. The "shot heard round the world" sounded at Old North Bridge and triggered the Revolutionary War. Nearby Walden Pond moved Henry David Thoreau to record profound observations on nature and mankind. Nathaniel Hawthorne, Ralph Waldo Emerson, and the Alcotts made their homes in Concord, nurtured by its ineffable energy.

The Hawthorne Inn offers guests the opportunity to discover Concord and perhaps to experience the force that so inspired America's Transcendentalists. Originally owned by Hawthorne himself, the property has a fascinating history. Good friend Bronson Alcott constructed a Bath House on the land just behind the inn and, using "sylvan architecture," created other elaborate structures made from forest finds. The Bath House was to

be his grandest building, the magnetic point of all his other artworks. Though the building no longer stands, trees planted by these famous neighbors bear silent testimony to its earlier presence. Across from the inn sits Hawthorne's home "Wayside." Grapevine Cottage, where the Concord grape was developed, is another close neighbor.

In the mid-1970s artist Gregory Burch was attracted to Concord and to this house, which was large enough to contain his painting and sculpture studio as well as rooms for wayfarers. He and his wife Marilyn offer guests the comforts of an impeccably maintained and antiques-filled home. Gregory's soapstone bas-relief carvings and energetic paintings, and Marilyn's beautifully designed quilts contribute, along with books of poetry and art, and Mayan and Inca artifacts, to make the Hawthorne Inn a very stimulating haven.

HAWTHORNE INN, 462 Lexington Rd., Concord MA 01742; (617) 369-5610; Gregory Burch and Marilyn Mudry, hosts. Charming inn on site steeped in American history. Open March through December. Five guest rooms, shared baths. Rates: $60 single, $80 double, $20 third person. Continental breakfast. No credit cards; no pets. Wide variety of restaurants within 10-minute drive. Equally wide variety of sports and spots of interest in this scenic country.

DIRECTIONS: from Rte. 128–95, take Exit 45 west for 3½ miles. Bear right at the single blinking light. Inn is one mile on left, across from "Wayside" (Hawthorne and Alcott home).

WINDAMAR HOUSE

Provincetown mix of antiques and art

At the tip of a twenty-five mile arc of beaches and windswept sand dunes, Provincetown, the terminus of Cape Cod, is a year-round resort of exceptional beauty. Summertime ushers in the carnival season. Two main thoroughfares, lined with art galleries, shops, museums, and restaurants, teem with tourists and sun worshippers. The contemplative beauty of the spring and fall attracts naturalists and artists. In winter, uncluttered by people and protected from Arctic temperatures by ocean currents, this spectacular landscape reveals its basic lines.

In any season Windamar House is a fine place to stay. Bette Adams and Muriel Goodwin's Cape colonial house sits in a quiet residential pocket just "this side" of Provincetown's commercial district. Windamar has a picket-fenced front yard, gardens, a terraced backyard filled with lawn furniture, and, most importantly, a private parking lot. In a town that can't expand geographically, all of the above are at a premium.

A guest suite.

The stairway leading to the second-floor guest rooms.

Inside, the second-floor bedrooms range from a tiny cubbyhole to a suite with cathedral ceiling and a wall of glass. Besides single rooms, two fully equipped apartments are available for longer stays. Original art fills all available walls throughout the house, and bedrooms are an eclectic mix of antiques and comfortable period pieces.

Though Muriel and Bette are always about, making sure the coffee pot is filled in the morning and seeing to the needs of their guests, they are not an intrusive presence. Free to barbecue in the backyard or sit for hours in the lounge (complete with "no-cook" kitchen), guests settle in and make themselves at home.

WINDAMAR HOUSE, 568 Commercial St., Provincetown, MA 02657; (617) 487-0599; Muriel Goodwin and Bette Adams, hostesses. Some French spoken. Two houses joined together in the quiet east end of Provincetown. Open all year. Six guest rooms, sharing baths, and two fully equipped apartments. Rates $32 to $55 main house, according to season and room; apartments $45 per night off season, two-night minimum, $395 per week in season; rates include continental breakfast. Excellent dining nearby. Children welcome; no pets; no credit cards. Provincetown offers incomparable natural setting, year-round recreation, birdwatching, whale-watching.

DIRECTIONS: Take Cape Hwy. (Rte. 6) to Provincetown. Take first exit to water and turn right on 6A. At 'V' in road bear left onto Commercial St. Windamar House is ¼ mile ahead on right. Boats and flights available from Boston.

BEECHWOOD

A classic Cape Cod getaway cottage

Turning onto the Old Kings Highway, strains of Patti Page singing "Old Cape Cod" suddenly come to mind. The road to Beechwood meanders along classic sand dunes, past traditional clapboard-and-shingle cottages partially obscured by graceful, weathered trees. Amidst all this beauty, Beechwood is an especially romantic house, a Victorian cottage colored in the softest shades of jade green, butter yellow, and muted brick. Shaded by century-old copper beech trees, Beechwood is a classic Cape Cod getaway.

This Greek Revival-Queen Anne-Eastlake hybrid—architecture atypical to the area, to say the least—couldn't rest in better hands. East coast natives Bea and Jeffrey Goldstein owned a Victorian antiques shop in southern California before returning East to Barnstable. The Goldsteins' trained eyes shy away from the heavy, nightmarish aspects of the Victorian age; they have instead decorated their rambling home with the finest standards of the period. Clean and beautiful lines,

intriguing colors, and old-fashioned romance delight the senses.

One favorite bedroom, often requested by honeymooners, contains a four-poster bed of such grand proportions, that many guests need a booster stool to clamber up and under the covers. Another bedroom is a pristine jewel: lace-edged white sheets and down comforter, a white wicker rocker, and lace curtains accent a shiny brass bed, marble fireplace and a ruby velvet rocking chair. In the high, peaked garret another room is found. Through a half-moon window, guests can gaze past the treetops to the neighboring dunes and water.

Barnstable is a quiet village centrally located to all points in the Cape. Comprised of private residences and containing an assortment of fine antiques shops, it is a wonderful place to catch the magical mood of Cape Cod—the stuff about which songs are written.

BEECHWOOD, 2839 Main St., Barnstable Village, MA 02630; (617) 362-6618; Bea and Jeffrey Goldstein, hosts. Some French and Spanish spoken. Victorian shingled house with large porch and tinted windows. Open all year. Five distinctive guest rooms, two with fireplaces, all private baths. Rates $75 to $95 per room, including light breakfast. Afternoon tea. Excellent seafood dining in area. No children; no pets; Visa/MasterCard. Cape Cod offers dunes, beaches, boating, antiques.

DIRECTIONS: take Rte. 6 (Mid-Cape Hwy.) to exit 6 and turn left onto Rte. 132. Drive to stop sign and turn right onto Main St. Inn is 1.17 miles further on right.

Left, high tea by the hearth.

RHODE ISLAND

THE OLD DENNIS HOUSE

Bed and breakfast in Newport

Newport is many things to many people, from sailing mecca to the site of architectural wonders, from peerless colonial structures to ostentatious turn-of-the-century palaces.

The oldest section of Newport, known as The Point, is a quiet neighborhood filled with vintage homes, many of which were built in the mid-1700s when Newport was a major port city second only to Boston. Though Newport never fully recovered from the crippling destruction of the British occupation in 1776, the charm of The Point survived. Situated on the oldest street in Newport, the Old Dennis House stands out among these gracious survivors. Built in 1740 by Captain John Dennis, it serves as rectory for St. John's Episcopal Church and is one of Newport's finest bed and breakfast establishments.

Reverend Henry D. Turnbull had been rector of St. John's for over twenty years when a bed and breakfast registry persuaded him to open the spacious third floor of the rectory to guests. Besides the pleasure of meeting interesting people and offering comfortable accommodations to weary wayfarers (certainly a work of mercy), upkeep of the rectory was erased from the parish budget!

Each guest room is simple and charming with lots of exposed brickwork, several working fireplaces, and an eclectic mix of antiques. Located several blocks from the hubbub of Thames Street and Brick Market Place, the Old Dennis House is convenient to the bustling waterfront but feels a world removed.

THE OLD DENNIS HOUSE, 59 Washington St., Newport, RI 02840; (401) 846-1324; Rev. Henry D. Turnbull, host. Three guest rooms plus luxury suite in adjoining building; all with private baths. Open year-round. Rates: double $65 in summer, $50 in winter. Continental breakfast. Checks accepted.

DIRECTIONS: from Connecticut, cross Newport Bridge and take downtown Newport exit; 200 ft. off exit, turn right at light onto Van Zandt Ave. Go 3 blocks to Washington St. and turn left. Inn is about 7 blocks. From Boston, follow signs to Goat Island. At causeway to island, go 2 blocks north on Washington to corner of Poplar St.

St. John's Episcopal Church and the Rectory.

First-floor formal parlor.

BRINLEY VICTORIAN INN

Unpretentious, well-tended, relaxed

On a quiet street off the beaten track, yet close to both the bustle of town and the mansions of Bellevue Avenue, the Brinley Victorian Inn is really two houses, a mansard-roofed Victorian frame and a smaller, adjoining counterpart. The parlor in the main house is formal and eye-pleasing, filled with Victorian settees, a rocker, and lace-draped tables, all in soft shades of green and cream. In the evening, guests congregate here, or in the game room at the rear of the house, comparing notes on the day's activities, preparing the next day's schedule, or relaxing over a game of cards. The overall atmosphere at the Brinley is unpretentious, friendly, well-tended, and relaxed.

The seventeen guest rooms are furnished with an easy mix of Victorian and contemporary pieces, and featured in each is one of owner Edwina Sebest's collection of antique miniature lamps and candlesticks. She and partner Amy Weintraub left high-powered jobs in Pittsburgh—Amy was a television writer and executive producer, Edwina a psychologist in private practice—to move to this city they both truly love. They operate a nursing home three blocks from the inn but are often at the Brinley to help out with chores and to visit with their guests.

THE BRINLEY VICTORIAN INN, 23 Brinley St., Newport, RI 02840; (401) 849-7645; Robert Matoes, host; Edwina Sebest and Amy Weintraub, owners. Open year-round; Seventeen guest rooms; seven with private baths. Two newly restored Victorian houses connected by walkway. Rates by room: winter, $45 to 50, summer, $50 to 75; $5 for 3rd person. Continental breakfast. No children under twelve; no pets; checks accepted. Extensive dining in area.

DIRECTIONS: from Newport/Jamestown bridge (Rte. 138), take downtown Newport exit. Go to second light and turn left on Touro. At second light, turn left on Kay, and then right on Brinley. From north, take Rte. 114 into downtown. At movie theaters, bear left onto Touro and repeat above directions.

OVERLEAF: *the elaborate gates to the Breakers, Newport's most famous summer cottage.*

SERVICE
ENTERANCE

Dining room and adjoining kitchen, featuring a Garland professional stove.

ELLERY PARK HOUSE

A home, not a business

Margo and Michael Waite opened their home to overnight guests in 1979 when volunteers were needed to house participants in a transatlantic sailboat race. The experience was so enjoyable and satisfying that the Waites have continued to offer accommodations for visitors to Newport.

As in the European tradition, the Ellery Park House is first and foremost a home, not a business. The atmosphere is intimate and private; the two guest rooms are immaculate and simply furnished. Named after the vest-pocket park that adjoins the property, this modest turn-of-the-century row house in the historic district of Newport is within walking distance of shops, restaurants, movie theaters, and the harbor.

Reflecting the Waite's appreciation for good food, developed over years of travel and through Michael's business (managing a fine local café-restaurant), the kitchen is well equipped with a professional Garland stove, a battery of copper kitchenware, and a collection of cookbooks. Breakfast can be had in the early morning before the Waites take off for work (Margo is associate publisher of a well-known sailing magazine) or later in the day via a thermos and securely wrapped homebaked goodies. Besides homemade breads and coffee cakes, breakfast includes orange juice squeezed fresh each day, and a variety of hot and bracing beverages, among them that rarity in American kitchens, fresh-brewed espresso.

ELLERY PARK HOUSE, 44 Farewell St., Newport, RI 02840; (401) 847-6320; Margo and Michael Waite, hosts. Cozy late-Victorian clapboard-and-shingle-home. Open year-round. Two guest rooms, shared bath. Rates: $45 per room. Continental breakfast. Children discouraged; no pets; smoking discouraged; checks accepted. Four blocks from waterfront; all the pleasures of Newport. Great dining in area.

DIRECTIONS: from Boston, take Rte. 114. into Newport past City Hall to Farewell St. Turn right; house is about 5 blocks on left. From Connecticut, take Rte. 138 over Jamestown–Newport Bridge. Take first exit off bridge; at bottom of ramp, turn right and go through 2 lights. At fork in road, bear right and take first left, and left again onto Farewell. Inn is at end of this block.

CONNECTICUT

RED BROOK INN

A colonial gem near Mystic Seaport

Sitting in a California Victorian house filled with a lifetime's collection of Early American antiques, Ruth Keyes came to the conclusion that she would never feel altogether at home in the West. So when husband Vern Sasek suggested she find them a house in New England, she didn't miss a beat. Within six months Ruth and Vern owned a beautiful 1770 colonial in the tiny village of Old Mystic, Connecticut.

The house has unusually high ceilings, fine original wrought iron hardware, and wide-plank pine floors. It is an architecturally pure house because, though occupied continually since the 1700s, it was never tampered with or modernized. In 1972, two restoration experts brought the house into the twentieth century without disturbing the character or the structure.

Under Ruth's guardianship, the Red Brook Inn is a colonial showcase. Her collection of furniture and artifacts perfectly complements both the lines and the spirit of the house. All of the rooms are filled with period antiques, from the second-floor bedrooms with their blanket chests, highboys, and early lighting devices, to the first-floor keeping room with its original cooking fireplace, beehive oven, and iron crane and cookware. Ruth and Vern did opt for sturdy reproduction bedsteads in the name of comfort and longevity.

A full breakfast, served on the long harvest table in the keeping room, might include quiche, baked or fresh fruit, eggs Benedict, walnut waffles, or berry pancakes.

THE RED BROOK INN, Box 237, Rte. 184 at Wells Rd., Old Mystic, CN 06372; (203) 572-0349; Ruth Keyes and Vern Sasek, hosts. Some Czech spoken. Colonial gem built around 1770. Open year-round. Four guest rooms; two with shared baths. Rates by room: May 15–Nov. 15, $75–85; Nov. 15–May15, $60–65. Full breakfast served. No pets; no smoking in rooms; Visa/MasterCard/American Express.

DIRECTIONS: take I-95 to exit 89 (Allyn St.); go north 1½ miles to light (Rte. 184 Gold Star Hwy.), Turn right and go east ⅓ mile. Inn is on left.

OVERLEAF: *part of the extensive collection of ships' figureheads in the Mystic Seaport museum.*

BISHOP'S GATE INN

A theatrical inn near the Goodspeed

Perched on the banks of the Connecticut River, the grand proportions of the Goodspeed Opera House rise in sharp contrast to the surrounding tiny town of East Haddam. The Goodspeed produces musical comedy revivals and one new production a year—including the birth of such hits as *Man of La Mancha, Shenandoah,* and *Annie.* The quality of these productions is such that this house has come to be considered an off-Broadway theater. Besides the Goodspeed, East Haddam is a romantic rural village tailor-made for getting away from it all. Such an escape is easily accomplished by private plane (the airstrip is next to the theater), by boat (the dock is across from the Goodspeed), and, of course, by car.

Bishop's Gate Inn, located in the center of town, is a gem, abetted by the exuberant spirit of owner Julie Bishop and the artful way she has decorated her bed and breakfast inn.

The Jenny Lind Room.

Entering her home, guests immediately come upon the breakfast room. Above the sturdy harvest table hangs a gallery of familiar faces—friends made during Julie's years of working with the Goodspeed actors, many of whom appear on television and in movies. Opposite, a cheering fire crackles in the hearth. Each bedroom is named, and each is decorated with a light hand. For example, the Jenny Lind room is all softness and roses with framed floral prints, rosebud wallpaper, working fireplace, and an antique spool bed draped with a creamy fishnet canopy. The Director's Suite contains part of Julie's stunning marquetry collection, including two oversize twin beds, a chest of drawers, and an arm chair. This suite is made even more dramatic with its beamed cathedral ceiling, private balcony, and "Hollywood" bathroom complete with double sinks, sauna, and sitting area.

Above, one of the exquisite pieces in the marquetry collection sets off some Fred Astair memorabilia. Left, friends of Julie who have acted at the nearby Goodspeed Opera House, which is shown OVERLEAF.

BISHOP'S GATE INN, Goodspeed Landing, East Haddam, CT 06423; (203) 873-1677; Julie Bishop, hostess. Colonial built in 1818 and filled with family antiques. Six guest rooms, including one large suite; two with shared baths. Open year-round; closed Mondays. Rates $55–80 single; $70–95 double: $10 additional person. No children under six, no pets; checks accepted. Hearty continental breakfast; picnic lunches can be arranged.

DIRECTIONS: from New York City, Providence, or Boston, take Connecticut Tnpke. (I-95) to exit 69 to Rte. 9. From Rte. 9, take exit 7 to East Haddam. Cross bridge and take Rte. 149 to crest of first hill. Inn driveway is on right.

ESSEX BED & BREAKFAST

A private home of impeccable taste

The Connecticut River is broad and shallow, flanked by wooded countryside and dotted with villages established three centuries ago. The character of these communities remains much as it has always been, since the days when the river was a major artery for the distribution of goods to the interior of New England.

Essex is among the most charming and popular of Connecticut's colonial villages. A major ship-building town in its day, the Continental Navy's first man-of-war, the *Oliver Cromwell*, was built here at the shipyard of Uriah and John Hayden.

The town is filled with antique and craft shops, and also museums. In the Museum of the Connecticut River Foundation, you'll see a life-size model of the first U.S. submarine (1775), complete with hand-crank propeller. The Valley Railroad operates two steam engine trains, which carry passengers to the town of Deep River where they can board a passenger boat to tour past Gillette Castle and the Goodspeed Opera House.

One of the most satisfying ways to enter into the spirit of the area is to stay in a private home. This contemporary Cape Cod shingle cottage, designed by its owner, is decorated with a fresh point of view and impeccable taste. Nestled in this verdant setting, guests may enjoy a dip in the pond or request that a private dinner be prepared by their talented hostess.

ESSEX. Contemporary, passive-solar Cape Cod house. Open year-round, except at Christmas. Three guest rooms, shared baths. Rates: $40 single, $50 double, $10 extra for child. Continental breakfast. No crib facilities for infants; no pets; smoking discouraged. Beaches, sailing, golf, tennis, summer theater, and New Haven nearby. *Represented by Bed and Breakfast Registry, St. Paul, MN; Covered Bridge Bed and Breakfast, West Cornwall, CT; and Nutmeg Bed and Breakfast, West Hartford, CT.*

Formerly the son's bedroom, now a bed and breakfast guest room.

WEST LANE INN

Sample the good life in a private mansion

A New England getaway close to city bustle, the West Lane Inn in historic Ridgefield, Connecticut, is just fifty miles from New York City. This bed and breakfast inn contains more rooms than most, so guests don't always share their morning muffin and coffee with owner Maureen Mayer. But they enjoy the solid comforts evident throughout this grand, early nineteenth-century mansion. Among the amenities generally found only in fine hotels are thick padded carpets and a double thickness of door between adjoining rooms, which helps maintain the prevailing sense of quiet and privacy. Bathrooms are equipped with heated towel racks, full-length mirrors, and, in some cases, bidets. An adjoining house, called the Cottage, contains suites with service kitchens and private decks that open onto a vast expanse of well-manicured lawn. A simple room service menu, an optional full breakfast, king and queen-size beds, a tennis court, and one-day laundry and dry cleaning service make the West Lane Inn a welcome haven for tired wayfarers and business travelers.

WEST LANE INN, 22 West Lane, Ridgefield, CT 06877; (203) 438-7323; Maureen Mayer, hostess. Former private mansion invites guests to sample the good life. Open all year. Fourteen guest rooms in main house, two with working fireplaces; six suites in rear cottage; all private baths. Rates $80 single, $90 double, including continental breakfast; full breakfast available for extra charge. Good dining in area. Children welcome, cribs and playpens available; no pets; major credit cards; no checks. Ridgefield offers Revolutionary War sites, tours, museums; cross-country and downhill skiing.

DIRECTIONS: from NYC, take the FDR to the Major Deegan to Saw Mill Pkwy. Stay on Saw Mill to end and exit onto Rte. 35 going east. Drive approximately 12 miles to Ridgefield. Inn is on Rte. 35.

Left, a cabinet filled with early American glass, pewter, and redware pottery. Above, a portrait of the son of the original owner hangs in the stairway.

BUTTERNUT FARM

An impressive, small museum

Butternut Farm in Glastonbury, Connecticut, is an especially fine example of pre-Revolutionary architecture. The oldest section of the house was built by Jonathan Hale in 1720, a well-to-do gentleman with an eye for fine moldings and a feel for proportion—rare commodities in early homes. By the mid-1700s, a keeping room, "borning room," buttery, and extra bedchambers were added as Hale's family grew.

Present owner Don Reid is a·faithful steward to this architectural gem. He loves early American antiques and has collected many excellent examples from the period, including an antique pencil post canopied bed, an exquisite cherry highboy, and pre-Revolutionary bottles and Bennington pottery marbles.

The keeping room has beams bedecked with drying herbs and flowers. An antique settle and variety of chairs surround the large hearth, whose magnitude is completely overshadowed by the second fireplace found in the adjoining dining room. This brick hearth, of mammoth proportions, is teamed up with an oversized antique dining table and bannister-back chairs. An oil painting of Jonathan Hale's son is prominently displayed.

Guest rooms upstairs are decorated with wing-back chairs, wooden chests, and antique hat-boxes. Museum quality, hand-hooked rugs brighten softly gleaming, wide-plank pine floorboards.

Don Reid is a soft-spoken and intellectual man who takes great pride in the home he has created. Continuously occupied since its construction, the house shares its charm with appreciative guests. A carefully tended museum of Americana, this inn is like another world—one that should be visited and revisited to enjoy its many facets.

BUTTERNUT FARM, 1654 Main St., Glastonbury, CT 06033; (203) 633-7179; Don Reid, host. Elegant house built in 1720, with a wealth of interesting architectural detail. Open year-round. Four guest rooms, shared baths. Rates: $35 single, $42 double. Continental breakfast. Checks accepted; no pets; smoking discouraged. Good dining in town and in adjoining Hartford.

DIRECTIONS: take I-84 or I-91 to Rte. 2 exit. Follow Rte. 2 and take exit 8; go right toward Glastonbury Center. Drive to Main St. and turn left. Drive 1.6 miles, and inn is on left.

NEW YORK

BAKER'S BED & BREAKFAST

One of the premier bed and breakfasts

Although "modernized" as far back as 1840, this stone farmhouse was not restored until 1980 when artist and antiques dealer Fran Sutherland and her professor husband Doug Baker directed all of their energy into establishing one of the premier bed and breakfast inns in New York State. The house is large enough to contain two living rooms and two dining rooms; one chamber is graced with a Count Rumford fireplace and another opens onto a gloriously sunny solarium-greenhouse, complete with hot tub. The five upstairs bedrooms are equally welcoming, furnished with fluffy comforters and delicate watercolor paintings created by the hostess. Board-and-batten bedroom doors have original iron strap hinges, typical of the hardware used in the Hudson Valley during the colonial era.

The Shawangunk Mountain ridge is a magnificent backdrop for the Baker's stone house. Cross-

The 1840 stone cottage.

country ski trails and hiking trails abound, and the variety and number of fine restaurants is extraordinary. This area has become a Mecca for serious epicures.

Two things in particular delight Fran about innkeeping: first, exchanging ideas with guests and sharing creative pursuits; and second, watching guests unwind and knowing that this mountain getaway provides an atmosphere in which guests can thoroughly relax and enjoy themselves.

BAKER'S BED AND BREAKFAST, RD 2, Box 80, Stone Ridge, NY 12484; (914) 687-9795; Fran Sutherland and Doug Baker, hosts. Five rooms and two shared baths in a 1700s stone house. Open all year. Rates: $58.00 single/double; includes an elegant breakfast of wonderful breads and creative egg specialties served from dawn to 9:30 A.M. Reservations and a two-night minimum required; overnight guests mid-week only. No children; no pets; no credit cards; checks accepted. Non-smokers preferred but a considerate smoker would be acceptable.

DIRECTIONS: New York State Thruway (I-87) to New Paltz, exit 18. Drive west on Route 299 into New Paltz, turning right onto Rte. 32. Head north for about 6 miles and turn left onto Rte. 213. Proceed through High Falls and turn left onto Rte. 209. Take the second left off Rte. 209, which is Old Kings Highway; Baker's is midway down the hill on the right.

Left, a breakfast view of the Shawangunk Valley. Above, hostess Fran Sutherland.

THE OLDE POST INN

Live music on weekends

Nestled on the banks of the Hudson River, the town of Cold Spring basks in the beauty of the Palisades across the water. This village is an interesting mix of "local color" and city folk who were lured to the town for its lovely architecture and glorious setting. Among such new residents are Carole Zeller and George Argila. Their home, The Olde Post Inn, sits on a prominent corner of Main Street, two blocks from the river, and is one of the most successful restorations in the village.

The first floor of this cozy bed and breakfast serves as breakfast room and sitting room. It has open beamwork, hardwood floors, an antique sideboard, comfortable furniture, and a wall of glass that faces the backyard and patio, washing the beautiful woodwork with soft light. Carole collects American crafts and sells them from her tiny store, a room in the front of the house, while George, a graduate of the Julliard School of Music,

has opened a small cabaret in the basement. In the process of converting this unused basement space, George and Carole discovered a beehive fireplace, which sets the tone for the tavern. With its own separate entrance, no traffic flows from tavern to inn, except for those guests who spend the evening listening to music. George and other gifted, local musicians play on weekends—and no heavy rock is allowed.

It seems that at least half of Cold Spring is composed of antiques shops and other interesting stores. Besides shopping, visitors can tour the Chapel of Our Lady, an 1834 Greek Revival chapel, which was reproduced in Currier and Ives prints over a century ago, and the elegant eighteenth-century mansion called Boscobel. A short drive away are the Franklin D. Roosevelt National Historic Site and the fifty-room Vanderbilt mansion.

THE OLDE POST INN, 43 Main St., Cold Spring, NY 10516; (914) 265-2510; Carole Zeller and George Argila, hosts. 1820 Federal-style inn was once a post office and customs house. Open all year. Four guest rooms decorated in simple American traditional, shared bath. Rates $50 per room, including continental breakfast with homemade breads. Excellent dining nearby. Older children welcome; no pets; Visa/MasterCard. Tavern downstairs features live music on weekend nights.

DIRECTIONS: from west side of Hudson take Palisades Pkwy. to Bear Mt. Bridge. Turn left on Rte. 9D and proceed into Cold Spring. Turn left at light onto Main St. From NYC, take Taconic Pkwy. to Rte. 301, Cold Spring exit.

Left, the view from the breakfast room into the living room.

The house is colorful, gay, and fanciful.

UJJALA'S BED & BREAKFAST

A bit of California in upstate New York

Ujjala's Bed and Breakfast vibrates with a California sensibility. Her charming Victorian frame cottage sits amidst a grove of apple, pear, and quince trees, and is painted in luscious hues of lilac, periwinkle, and plum. Ujjala renovated her home and added skylights, contemporary stained glass, lots of plants, whimsical ceramics, and flowers.

The focus at Ujjala's is on health. With a background in "body therapy"—Shiatsu and deep-relaxation therapy—she has given courses in stress management to university students and corporate business people, and she was filmed for the television special "The Body Human." Ujjala is also an able cook who specializes in "vegetarian gourmet" cuisine. Her full breakfast includes homemade whole grain breads, fresh fruits, and eggs, and she goes out of her way to accommodate people on special diets. If you've always wanted to cleanse your system with a fast or a special diet, a stay at Ujjala's may be in order. Link a well-balanced and healthful diet with Ujjala's therapy and you can come away from this bed and breakfast feeling like a brand new person.

UJJALA'S BED AND BREAKFAST, 2 Forest Glen Rd., New Paltz, NY 12561; (914) 255-6360; Ujjala Schwartz, hostess. Open all year. Four guest rooms and one warm-weather studio, shared bath. Rates $40 to $50 double, including breakfast. Afternoon tea and coffee, sherry in winter. Excellent dining nearby. No children; no pets; smoking discouraged; no credit cards. Inn offers exercise and relaxation therapy programs.

DIRECTIONS: from N.Y. State Thruway, take New Paltz Exit 18. Go left on Rte. 299 into town and turn left at light onto Rte. 208 S. Drive 3½ miles, passing Dressel Farm on right, take second right onto Forest Glen Rd. Ujjala's is driveway on left.

THE GOLDEN EAGLE INN

An idyllic spot on the mighty Hudson

The location of The Golden Eagle is idyllic; the yard sweeps gently to the edge of the mighty Hudson. This stretch of the river is especially arresting, for across the way, built on a towering granite cliff, sits West Point Military Academy in grey gothic grandeur.

The inn is a lovely, soft red brick, three-story building. Embellished with a broad veranda, it feels like a transplant from a warmer climate. Inside, the rooms are decorated with an eye to incorporating bright and pleasing color. The focal point of one large suite is a half-canopied bed

Left, the Golden Eagle, to which you can travel by train, seaplane, or auto. Above, much attention has been lavished on the guest rooms.

strewn with white calla lilies on a peach background. Upstairs, rooms vary from spring bouquet colors of yellow, green, and pink to a lucious blend of blues, purples, and rose. George and Stephanie Templeton spent years in the design trade, and their light, professional touch works well. George is also an accomplished watercolorist, whose paintings brighten the walls of the parlor, breakfast room (used only when the weather prohibits dining on the veranda), and many of the bedrooms. Besides the continental breakfast of fresh fruit, croissants, and tea or coffee, the Templetons offer luncheon on the veranda during the warm months of the year. The menu might include overstuffed "riverboat" sandwiches, quiche, fresh fruit plates, soup, "the best chocolate cake in the world," and George's secret recipe, a drink known as "fresh fruit café."

The minute town of Garrison is dominated by the train station. Visitors from New York City need not bring a car. They can simply catch a train from Grand Central Station, which drops them off close to the inn's front door. Trains are available to take diners into Cold Spring in the evening and return them to the comforts of the inn afterwards.

THE GOLDEN EAGLE INN, Garrison's Landing, NY 10524; (914) 424-3067; George and Stephanie Templeton, hosts. Federal-style building, built in 1848 as hotel for visitors to West Point. Open most of year; closed for spring vacations. Six guest rooms, one a suite with private, handicap-accessible entrance. Private baths. Rates by room: $65–75; $15 for third person ($10 during week). Reservations mandatory; advance reservation with check only. Children discouraged and not accepted on weekends; no pets. Continental breakfast. Variety of restaurants within 15-minute drive. Museums, hiking. canoeing, vineyards, West Point nearby.

DIRECTIONS: from south, take Palisades Pkwy. to Bear Mountain Bridge. Cross bridge and take Rte. 9D to junction of Rte. 403. Turn left onto Rte. PC-12 toward river. Follow road to stop sign. Turn left over small bridge and turn left. Inn is 75 feet on right. From Cold Spring, take Rte. 9D to junction of Rte. 403. Turn right (PC-12) and follow directions above. Note: Inn can be reached by train from Grand Central Station, by boat on the Hudson, or by seaplane, with mooring at adjacent Highland Yacht Club.

PENNSYLVANIA

29 SOUTH CEDAR

In picturesque Lancaster County

Lancaster County is a crazy quilt of diversity, famed for Pennsylvania Dutch hospitality and towns with names like Paradise, Bird-In-Hand, and Eden, where the Old Order Amish with their horse-and-buggy travel and plain dress contrast so startlingly with the modern world. Driving past neat Amish farms, with windmills spinning and men plowing behind draft horses, the only lines you'll see that run to the farmhouse are those that support a day's wash. Old Order Amish do not use electricity or own automobiles.

The town of Lititz, just north of Lancaster, was founded in the eighteenth century as a Moravian religious community. Besides its Moravian past, Lititz is the home of the country's first candy-makers, Wilbur Chocolates, and the Sturgis Pretzel House, makers of the first American pretzel.

Centrally located one block from the main street, 29 Cedar Street offers all the comforts of home to visitors touring the area. Alice Gardner is an inveterate collector, and her home is filled with antiques and family mementos that create a warm atmosphere. Besides serving a full and varied breakfast, each morning a hot thermos of tea or coffee is delivered to the bedroom door.

29 SOUTH CEDAR, 29 S. Cedar St., Lititz, PA 17543; (717) 627-1080; Alice Gardner, hostess. Open year-round. Two bedrooms rented as a suite to never more than one party. Private bath. Rates: $45 for double, $55 with second bedroom or third person. Full breakfast served. Good selection of restaurants in Lancaster. No children under six, no pets; checks accepted.

DIRECTIONS: take Penn. Tnpke. to exit 21. Go south on Rte. 222 and take Brownsville exit. Turn right on Rte. 772 west into Lititz. Turn left onto S. Cedar at the post office. House is 1 block on right, opposite school.

Left, above, Amish attending a popular farm auction near Intercourse, PA. Left, below, a car of the famous Strasburg railroad. Above, one of the 29 South Cedar guest rooms.

Above, handmade beds and quilts in the guest rooms. Right, the first-floor breakfast room.

SMITHTON

Pennsylvania Dutch hospitality

In the mid-1700s Henry and Susana Miller were devout members of the Ephrata Community, a Protestant monastic religious group founded by charismatic leader Johann Conrad Beissel. As "outdoor members," the Millers lived by a more relaxed discipline than the majority of disciples, who were celibate and ascetic. The Millers' home, a sturdy stone structure that served as a tavern and stagecoach stop, sat on a hill overlooking the Community Cloister. The Cloister was a remarkably beautiful group of medieval German buildings constructed along the banks of the Cocalico Creek, where Beissel and his followers lived and worked. Although the community of believers declined over the years, the Cloister remains—as does the Millers' home, which is now an inn called Smithton.

Smithton is a warm and welcoming home, and Dorothy Graybill, a Lancaster County native, is the gracious hostess. In this inn guests are steeped in two centuries of history while treated to the the true spirit of Pennsylvania Dutch hospitality. Throughout the house, from the airy kitchen and adjoining dining room to the deluxe, two-story suite complete with Jacuzzi bath, they will enjoy the special attention that is given to wood, from handmade beds and Windsor chairs to hand-fashioned latches and hinges, their design taken from a Cloister pattern. The focal point of each bedroom is the traditional bright and cheerful, handstitched quilt—made by one of the local Mennonite ladies, of course. Extra-large, square down pillows, perfect props for a good read in bed, and soft flannel nightshirts hanging behind each door are just two of many thoughtful and creative touches. Each morning a full breakfast is served by Dorothy, who is assisted by a "plain person," local parlance for the Mennonite and Amish people.

SMITHTON, 900 W. Main St., Ephrata, PA 17522; (717) 733-6094; Dorothy Graybill, hostess. Pennsylvania Dutch spoken. Rustic stone house built in 1762. Four guest rooms plus one suite, private and shared baths. Open year-round. Rates: $35 to $75 rooms, $105 suite, $10 third person (no fee for infants). Continental breakfast. Interesting choice of restaurants in area. Children and pets accepted; checks accepted; must prepay in full.

DIRECTIONS: from north or south, take Rte. 222 to the Ephrata exit. Turn west on Rte. 322 (Ephrata's Main Street) and drive 2½ miles to Smithton.

Guest rooms, left, are fresh and cheerful, and the main living room, above, is calm and elegant.

BARLEY SHEAF FARM

Romance and charm for blithe spirits

A sense that all's right with the world is the hallmark of the best inns. Barley Sheaf Farm in Bucks County emanates that wonderful feeling of security and comfort.

The property has attracted blithe and sophisticated spirits throughout its life, most notably when it was owned by playwright George S. Kaufman, and weekend guests included Moss Hart, Lillian Hellman, S.J. Perlman, and Alexander Woollcott.

Today, Ann and Don Mills' guests may stay in the farmhouse or in one of three bedrooms in the converted ice house. Bedrooms in the main house vary in size, but total charm is assured in each. A two-room suite furnished with an impressive brass sleigh bed, broad and comfortable upholstered couch, working fireplace, and French doors with handpainted privacy screen is the largest bedchamber. The separate ice house, comprising a living room with three very individual, country-style bedrooms, is tailor-made for couples traveling together.

A great percentage of the foodstuffs for a truly splendid breakfast come from the farm; the Millses raise chickens, keep bees, and harvest a large crop of raspberries each year. A puffy soufflé made from fresh eggs, buttery biscuits dripping with Barley Sheaf honey, feather-light pancakes and fresh raspberry sauce garnished with nutmeg-flecked sour cream, a homemade sausage ring, apple crêpes filled with cheese, nuts, and raisins and napped with homemade apple syrup, a sour cream coffee cake—need one say more to describe total satisfaction?

BARLEY SHEAF FARM, Box 10, Rte. 202, Holicong, PA 18928; (215) 794-5104; Ann and Don Mills, and Don Mills, Jr., hosts; Mary Scalzo, manager. French spoken by Ann. Open March through last weekend before Christmas. Six guest rooms in main house, plus three in cottage; private baths. Rates: $50 to $90, $15 per extra person. Full breakfast served. Wide selection of restaurants in area. No children under eight; no pets; checks accepted.

DIRECTIONS: from Philadelphia, take I-95 north to exit 332 (Newtown). Turn left at exit and drive to third light, turning right onto Rte. 532. Take first left at Goodnoes Restaurant and then turn left again onto Rte. 413 north. Follow 413 for about twelve minutes and turn right at intersection of Rte. 202. Farm is on the right about a five-minute drive on 202.

BRIDGETON HOUSE

French doors onto the Delaware

Bridgeton House sits on the banks of the Delaware River. This is an enviable position, for while many Bucks County hostels advertise proximity to the river as a drawing card, few can truly say the river is their backyard. Beatrice and Charles Briggs restored their seven-room inn with an eye to incorporating the river by installing French doors and laying a pebble patio that sweeps to the edge of the riverbank.

With Charles' talent as a master carpenter and Bea in charge of interior design, the Briggses completely renovated and decorated what was a derelict building, an eyesore caught between the bridge and the road. Today, Bridgeton House feels like a cross between American country-naive and French provincial style. Bea uses soft color throughout, Williamsburg shades of faded cobalt, muted mulberry, and clotted cream. Thick rag rugs and a collection of antique Oriental area rugs accent painted hardwood floors. Fine bed

linens and puffy comforters please the eye and assure the traveler of a comfortable night's sleep.

Bridgeton House is a casual, but sophisticated environment. Before becoming innkeepers, Bea and Charles worked in Bucks County inns and restaurants, and their years of experience show. Always available, but never intrusive, Bea sets a relaxing tone. She loves to cook and often can be found in the inn's beautiful kitchen, which opens onto the entry hall and adjoining dining room.

Outside the door, the Delaware River affords many diversions, starting with its lovely sixty-mile towpath, which is perfect for hiking, cross-country skiing, picnicking, and jogging. Canoeing, fishing, and tubing enthusiasts proclaim the Delaware to be among the East Coast's finest rivers.

BRIDGETON HOUSE, River Rd., Upper Black Eddy, PA 18972; (215) 982-5856; Charles and Beatrice Briggs, hosts. Built in 1836 as a private residence, this home also once served as a bakery and candy store. Open year-round. Seven guest rooms, all with private baths. Rates: on weekends by room $70–80, during week $10 less per room; single rate during week $20 less per room. Full breakfast. Good restaurants close by. Children discouraged; no pets; smoking discouraged; Visa/MasterCard/American Express/checks. Swimming, tubing on Delaware River, tow path, fishing, biking, antiques.

DIRECTIONS: from Philadelphia, take I-95 north to New Hope/Yardley exit. Follow signs north to New Hope. Continue north on Rte. 32, 18 miles to inn.

The elegant entry hall.

Conversation area around the hearth.

PINEAPPLE HILL

Intimacy and comfort in New Hope

The streets of New Hope are thickly lined with chic shops and restaurants that cater to the great flow of tourists visiting Bucks County each year; this bustling village is the county's hub. Just four miles from New Hope's commercial center, Pineapple Hill offers the intimacy and comfort of a family home with the convenience of being close to everything.

The first floor of Mary and Stephen Darlingtons' house is furnished in a simple manner appropriate to its age, *circa* 1800. In the breakfast parlor a trestle table is illuminated by a tin chandelier fitted with candles. Wing chairs and a camelback sofa form a conversation area around the hearth, where fires blaze on cool days. On the wall are hung artifacts from the Darlington dairy business. Stephen's family owns a William Penn land-grant dairy farm, and remnants from its heyday— commercial signs for Darlington table butter and

even a Darlington train station sign—reflect the glory of this once-thriving family business. Plain hardwood floors and a wall case filled with lovely old pewter complete the mood of simple quality.

The house was built in several sections, and four antiques-filled guest rooms are thus divided, two in the second-floor wing and two under the third-floor eaves. This layout makes it easy to convert the rooms into two separate suites that are perfect for families or for two couples.

One of the most striking features of Pineapple Hill is its use of the stone ruins in the backyard. Where once a barn stood there is now a swimming pool, made private by the charming remains of the barn's foundations.

PINEAPPLE HILL, River Rd., RD 3, Box 34C, New Hope, PA 18939; (215) 862-9608; Mary and Stephen Darlington, hosts. Some German spoken. Open year-round. Four guest rooms, all doubles. Rates: $50 a room, continental breakfast and afternoon tea served; special diets accommodated upon advance notice. Accommodations for only one child available (inquire ahead); no pets; smoking in parlor only; American Express/checks. Swimming pool on premises, excellent dining in area.

DIRECTIONS: from Philadelphia, take I-95 to New Hope/ Yardley exit. Drive north on Taylorsville Rd. to junction with Rte. 32. Inn is 100 yards north on 32, second driveway on right. From New York City, take New Jersey Tnpke. south to exit 10. Take I-287 north to Rte. 22, and 22 west to Rte. 202. Take 202 south to New Hope exit (first in Penn.). Drive south through New Hope on River Rd. (Rte. 32); continue 4 miles out of New Hope; inn is on left.

NEW JERSEY

CHESTNUT HILL ON THE DELAWARE

Old-fashioned and very romantic

Visitors to Linda and Rob Castagna's home, Chestnut Hill, are enveloped by the warmth of the atmosphere and the beauty of the setting on the banks of the Delaware.

Bedrooms are old-fashioned and very romantic, thanks to Linda's gift for color and design and her many small touches. On the door of each room hangs a delicate wreath, and inside a handcrafted cloth basket is filled with fresh fruit in season. One room, entitled Peaches and Cream, is an aptly named chamber with soft peach-striped wallpaper, puffy peach comforter draped with a lace coverlet, and an oak chest of drawers and armoire. The Pineapple Room, which was the servants quarters, is roomy and private at the rear of the second floor. Decorated in cream, yellows,

and greens, the room offers a bed dressed with a luxurious Welsh duvet and a wall of built-in drawers and cabinets in which hides a television. Bayberry features a bay window fitted with original shutters and is decorated in sprightly primary shades taken from colors in the bed's antique quilt.

Up a steep staircase to the attic suite, the bridal favorite, guests are in a world of their own. One bedroom is named Teddy's Room and contains several furry bears and a Little Golden Book of the *Three Bears* tale. Against a warm and rosy red print wallpaper, white eyelet and ruffled bedclothes look crisp and inviting. The bathroom, which displays beautiful Mexican tile work, overlooks the swift-flowing Delaware.

CHESTNUT HILL ON THE DELAWARE, 63 Church St., Milford, NJ 08848; (201) 995-9761; Linda and Rob Castagna, hosts. Victorian house built in 1860, with gallery/gift shop on premises. Open year-round. Five guest rooms, shared and private baths. Rates: $55 to $60 singles, $80 suite. Full breakfast served. Excellent dining in area. No pets; checks accepted.

DIRECTIONS: from Milford, turn right at light and right again on Church St. (1 street before Delaware River bridge). Turn left into dead-end, which is Chestnut Hill's parking area.

Left, a photograph of the hosts and their son, dressed in the period clothes that they love to collect.

WOOLVERTON INN

A grand setting near Bucks County

The two most striking characteristics of the Woolverton Inn are its grand situation and the relaxed and flexible atmosphere. The building is a large and impressive manor house of undressed stone; the original section was built around 1793, and the mansard-roofed third floor, decorative iron grillwork, and long sweeping porches were added in 1876.

The setting is lovely. Fully grown sugar maples stand like sentinels in the sweeping front lawn, and in autumn their foliage is breathtakingly brilliant. Behind the house, sheep graze on the rolling meadow that stretches as far as the eye can see. The grounds are spacious enough to feel isolated from the world, though the inn is quite close to the village of Stockton.

The furnishings of the house—a fine selection of antiques and assorted comfortable easy chairs and sofas—blend compatibly with the elegance of the formal dining room, the rusticity of wide-plank oak floors and narrow hallways.

Woolverton emanates an easy-going attitude of laissez-faire. This tone is exemplified in the breakfast regimen. Guests may take this meal when they want and where they want, be it in their room at 7 A.M. or under a maple tree at 3 P.M.

One note: the Woolverton ownership recently changed hands. Though the new innkeepers are adopting the inn, attitudes and all, there will doubtless be changes in the upcoming years. Nothing, however, can change the basic charm of the setting or lovely lines of the house.

WOOLVERTON INN, Box 233, R.D. 3, Stockton, NJ 08559: (609) 397-0802; Gary Wheeler, host; Sara Burns, assistant. French spoken. Gracious colonial stone manor house on ten acres of land. Open year-round. Ten guest rooms, including one two-bedroom suite, all with private baths. Rates: $55 to 95. Full continental breakfast, afternoon tea. Excellent dining in area. No children under thirteen; no pets; American Express/checks. Endless possibilities for recreation in scenic Bucks County.

DIRECTIONS: from Philadelphia, take I-95 north and cross Delaware River to N.J. Take first exit in N.J. (Rte. 29) and follow 29 north through Lambertville to Stockton. Take Rte. 523 for ⅛ mile and turn left on Woolverton Rd. Inn is second drive on right. From New York City, take N.J. Tnpke. south to Exit 10. Then take Rte. 287 north for 14 miles to Rte. 22 exit west. Continue on 22 for 2½ miles and take Rte. 202 exit south for 25 miles to Lambertville exit just before Delaware River Bridge. Take Rte. 29 north to Stockton.

YORK STREET HOUSE

The most formal and elegant of all

Because it was built by a wealthy coal magnate as a lavish anniversary gift for his wife, the York Street House is one of the most formal and elegant inns in the Bucks County area. George Massey spared no expense and in 1909 spent $65,000 on his home. On the first floor he installed three beautiful Mercer tile fireplaces—one in the formal parlor, one in the dining room, and a third in the cherrywood-paneled library. Leaded glass wall cases, colorful stained-glass windows, and a Waterford crystal chandelier were a few of the elegant details. The second floor was given over to bedchambers and dressing rooms for the Masseys, and servants quarters and a sewing room occupied the third floor. Such was the spending and splendor of the house, that *House and Garden* magazine featured the Massey Mansion in its December 1911 issue.

The Teddy Roosevelt Room.

Before its life as an inn, the house was used as a designer showcase. One of the more interesting and successful designs—a bedroom decorated with tiny leopard-spot cloth wallcovering, a Victorian bedroom set painted the buttery shades of tans and browns, an elegant checked wool quilt, and pinstriped sheeting—is atypical, masculine in feel, and goes by the name Teddy Roosevelt. More typical are the bedrooms dressed in Laura Ashley prints that create a light and charming mood. Each of the third-floor bedrooms has that cozy feeling that sloping ceilings and dormer windows give to any space.

The downstairs parlor is a soft mix of palest lavender walls accented by white moldings and furnishings in shades of green and rose. A selection of small oil paintings adorn the walls, and the Waterford chandelier hangs in its original spot. Across the hall the dark cherrywood depths of the library play a contrasting role.

YORK STREET HOUSE, 42 York St., Lambertville, NJ 08530; (609) 397-3007; Cornelius Peck, host. Georgian Revival home built in 1909, with carriage house and antiques shop in rear. Open year-round. Seven guest rooms, shared and private baths. Rates: $60 to $90. Full breakfast served. Excellent dining in area. No children under twelve; no pets; checks accepted. All the pleasures of Bucks County.

DIRECTIONS: from Philadelphia, take I-95 north and cross Delaware River. Take Lambertville exit (Rte. 29) north to York St. and turn left.

Left, Joy Peto Smiley, John Peto's granddaughter, in the studio. Above, some of John Peto's paintings, including a self-portrait on the easel.

THE STUDIO OF JOHN F. PETO

A secluded artist's studio

Gifted in the art of still life, John F. Peto, who lived during the latter half of the nineteenth century, was an artist whose talent was to go unrecognized in his lifetime. Throughout his career, he was unfavorably compared to friend and fellow painter William Michael Harnett. In 1950 the tide began to turn when the Brooklyn Museum mounted Peto's first major exhibition. Thirty-three years later when the National Gallery of Art organized a retrospective that traveled from Washington, D.C. to the Amon Carter Museum in Fort Worth, Texas, Peto finally emerged as a major American painter, now considered by many to be a far greater talent than Harnett.

Peto lived his life in virtual seclusion in Island Heights, a quiet village along the New Jersey shore, in a house he built overlooking the Tom's River. He first designed a studio for himself, a spacious and high-ceilinged room with white stuccoed fireplace, white walls, and "Peto red" wainscoting. He then built his home, including seven bedrooms, around the studio.

Granddaughter Joy Peto Smiley, as ebullient as her forebears were reclusive, has opened her grandfather's home and studio to overnight guests. Rooms are furnished much as they always have been, unpretentious with an eclectic mix of beds, chest, and chairs. In the common rooms hang reproductions of Peto's most famous paintings, and the studio holds a small selection of his original works.

Whether dining on Joy's "ethereal eggs," fresh fruit, and hot popovers, or walking through historic Island Heights, the studio, filled with the strong and quiet presence of John Peto, is the most memorable part of a stay.

THE STUDIO OF JOHN F. PETO, 102 Cedar Ave., Island Heights, NJ 08732; (201) 270-6058; Joy Peto Smiley, hostess. Open year-round. Seven guest rooms, shared baths. Rates: $45 single, $55 double. Hearty breakfast served. Variety of restaurants, including a wonderful seafood eatery, in the area. No children; no pets; Visa/MasterCard/American Express/checks.

DIRECTIONS: take Garden State Pkwy. to exit 82 east. Pass through six stoplights. Two blocks further, turn right onto Central Ave. and drive ¼ mile; halfway up the first hill, turn left onto Summit. Drive 4 blocks and turn right onto Cedar. Inn is 2 blocks on left (look for sign "The Studio").

The largest, most imposing guest room.

THE NORMANDY INN

Gracious privacy a block from the beach

Of all the seaside villages that attract vacationers to the New Jersey shore, none is more gracious than Spring Lake. Bypassed by the teeming hordes who populate streets, casinos, and beaches of larger resorts, Spring Lake emanates a special grace particular to communities made up of broad avenues lined with grand, tree-shaded "cottages."

Built in 1888 as a private residence and expanded in 1916, The Normandy Inn, which comprises eighteen bedrooms, sits one block from the beach. Size alone makes the Normandy feel like a small resort hotel, though innkeepers Susan and Michael Ingino, who live in the house year-round with daughter Beth, maintain a warm and homey atmosphere.

Breakfast at this inn is especially generous and delicious. Each morning guests seat themselves in the large dining room—a room of such scale that young Beth dreams of converting it into her own private skating rink. The written menu offers many choices. Besides the requisite juices, hot beverages, and cold cereals, the Inginos serve real Irish porridge, four types of pancakes, two sorts of French toast, six varieties of eggs, four breakfast meats, and Michael's fresh-baked muffins or soda bread. Breakfast is Michael's favorite meal, and as a chef, he sees to it that guests need eat but a sparing lunch.

The Inginos are avid collectors of Victoriana and are slowly furnishing each room with antiques from the period. Rooms vary in size, but each is clean and very comfortable.

THE NORMANDY INN, 21 Tuttle Ave., Spring Lake, NJ 07762; (201) 449-7172; Michael and Susan Ingino, hosts. Italianate Victorian home near beach offers casual comfort and thoughtful amenities. Open all year. Eighteen guest rooms in house, two over garage, most with private baths. Rates $55 to $80 in season, $43 to $60 off season, double occupancy. Includes full breakfast. Good dining throughout area. Children who enjoy quietude welcome; no pets; smoking discouraged; no credit cards. Area offers beach, horseback riding, antiques, state park.

DIRECTIONS: from north, take Garden State Pkwy. to exit 98 (Rte. 34). Proceed south on 34 to traffic circle. Drive ¾ way around and turn right on Rte. 524 east. Cross Rtes. 35 and 71. Rte. 524 then becomes Ludlow Ave. Proceed to end of Ludlow and turn right onto Ocean Ave., then first right onto Tuttle. From south, take Garden State Pkwy. to exit 98 (Rte. 38 E). Cross Rte. 18 and turn right at next traffic light onto New Bedford Rd. Take sharp left at second stop sign (Rte. 524) and proceed as above.

CAPTAIN MEY'S INN

Graced with exquisite detail

America's oldest seaside resort, Cape May conjures by its very name, visions of gingerbread and wedding-cake castles-by-the-sea. Protected from progress by the Pine Barrens and acres of wetlands plus miles of fertile fields that yield succulent Jersey produce, the village retains much of the charm of centuries past.

One advantage for today's visitor is the abundance of lovely bed and breakfast establishments, each quite different in spirit and temperament. The three on these pages are a sampler; it would take weeks to exhaust all the possibilities.

Captain Mey's Inn is named for Cornelius Jacobsen Mey, of the Dutch East Indies Company, who explored the area in 1621 and served as its namesake. This solidly built, late-Victorian mansion is decorated like an old-fashioned valentine. Voluminous lace curtains and lacey privacy screens,

Two details of the foyer and parlor.

called *horretjes*, frame the windows. A china cabinet filled with innkeeper Carin Fedderman's collection of antique Delftware, family portraits, a nineteenth-century bible, antique pewter and copper, and abundant knickknacks and bric-a-brac fill the first-floor parlor and dining room. Carin is from Holland, and her Dutch heritage, linked with that of Captain Mey, inspired her and partner Milly La Canfora to create an inn reminiscent of her home. Many small touches—a small Persian rug on the clawfoot dining table; a plush, purse-like tea cozy; and the decorative *horretjes*—are found in many Dutch homes and add a distinctive European flavor. The house itself is graced with exquisite detail from three signed Tiffany stained-glass windows in the inner foyer to leaded, diamond-paned, ripple glass windows that glisten in the wide bay in the dining room.

CAPTAIN MEY'S INN, 202 Ocean St., Cape May, NJ 08204; (609) 884-7793/9637; Carin Fedderman and Milly La Canfora, hostesses. Dutch spoken and some French, German, Spanish, Italian. Open all year. Eight guest rooms, private and shared baths. Rates $50 to $85 double, varying with season and amenities; includes full breakfast served by candlelight. Afternoon tea. Excellent dining nearby. No children under twelve; no pets; smoking restricted; no credit cards. Cape May offers beaches, sight-seeing, antiques.

DIRECTIONS: take causeway bridge (Lafayette St.) to second light and turn left onto Ocean St. Inn is 1½ blocks ahead on right.

A Dutch tea cozy.

THE QUEEN VICTORIA

Imposing Victorian on Cape May

The Queen Victoria ranks among the best of Cape May's many distinctive bed and breakfast inns. It towers on the corner of Ocean Street and Columbia Avenue, a dramatic green and maroon gingerbread cottage. Owners Joan and Dane Wells are perfectly suited to the task of pampering this Victorian lady. Before beginning a career as an innkeeper, Joan was curator of the Molly Brown House in Denver as well as the executive director of The Victorian Society. Both positions required a dedication to the preservation of old houses, a labor Joan truly loves. Dan is the perfect counterpart. Though a tinkerer and hardware store aficionado, his professional background in retailing keeps the inn's business side on an even keel.

One of the most attractive and interesting rooms in the entire house is the front parlor, which is filled with the Wellses' Arts and Crafts furniture collection—that wonderfully subdued offspring of the gaudy Victorian age.

Bedrooms come in many shapes and sizes. On the first floor the Queen Victoria room handily houses a massive armoire, tufted couch, king-size bed, and petit point chairs. Several rooms on the second floor and all on the third are diminutive and charming. The Wellses carefully selected wallpapers to suit the spirit of Victoriana, each with jewel-like hues and intricate patterns.

Though Cape May is a wonderful place to visit, no matter the season, the Wellses favorite time of year is Christmas. To make the season more joyous, they organize caroling, fireside readings from Dickens, and workshop sessions devoted to planning the Victorian Christmas dinner and decorating the Victorian home.

THE QUEEN VICTORIA, 102 Ocean St., Cape May, NJ 08204; (609) 884-8702; Dane and Joan Wells, hosts. French and some Spanish spoken. Open all year, minimum stays vary seasonally. Twelve guest rooms, private and shared baths. Rates $52 to $90 according to size and amenities (rates lower off season), including full breakfast served buffet style. Afternoon tea. Excellent dining nearby. No toddlers; no pets; smoking restricted; Visa/MasterCard.

DIRECTIONS: take Garden State Pkwy. to Cape May, where it becomes Lafayette St. Turn left at second stoplight (Ocean St.) and proceed three blocks to inn, on right.

One of host Spurgeon Smith's woodcarvings welcomes guests to the dining room.

THE MANOR HOUSE

Built in 1906 as a wedding gift

The foyer of The Manor House, with patterned chestnut wainscoting, a circular windowseat, lace-draped table, and stained-glass window, sets a mood of warmth and welcome. But what elevates this bed and breakfast a degree above the typically wonderful inn are the extraordinary woodcarvings that fill the house. A genius with wood, innkeeper Spurgeon Smith is able to bring wooden scupture to life and reveal the beautiful grain in each piece of wood. His special subjects are wildlife and mothers with their babies, many touched with a quirky sense of humor. Joyce Smith also has an exceptional eye for beautiful things and collects antique bisque dolls and hand-stitched quilts. The dolls fill a large glass case in the dining room, while the quilts fairly glow from each guest bed.

Besides the air of warmth and romance, a strong sense of whimsey permeates this house. Each morning, melodious tunes from the Smiths' computerized player piano herald that breakfast is soon to begin. The setting for this meal, which is served in the formal dining room, is sumptuous: sterling silver, fine china, and heirloom cut glass. In the evening the Smiths' might display the piano's classical skills. The sound is so true that on balmy days when open windows transport sound, passers-by have been known to applaud.

This three-story shingle "cottage" is filled with family heirlooms, from a handpainted wardrobe in Room 2 to a handcarved bedstead in Room 5. In the downstairs parlor a suede-bound book of hand-penned poems makes for fascinating reading. The poems are those of the young woman for whom this house was built as a wedding present in 1906. Her poetry is filled with the people and the feelings that populated her home.

THE MANOR HOUSE, 612 Hughes St., Cape May, NJ 08204; (609) 884-4710; Joyce and Spurgeon Smith, hosts. Colonial Revival shingled "cottage" open April through October. Ten guest rooms, shared and private baths. Rates $60 to $85 double, including full breakfast. Afternoon tea. Excellent dining nearby. No children under twelve; no pets; no smoking; no credit cards.

DIRECTIONS: take Garden State Pkwy. to its southernmost point and continue straight ahead on Lafayette St. Drive about one mile to Franklin St. and turn left. Drive two blocks and turn right onto Hughes St. Manor House is 1½ blocks ahead on left.

DELAWARE

Bed and breakfast and fine museums

Although most Americans don't think of Wilmington when they want to "get away from it all," it is the site of two of the finest museums in the country. Most famous and spectacular is Winterthur, home of Henry Francis Du Pont, who began collecting distinctive American decorative arts in 1923. He spent thirty years gathering the finest examples of furniture, fixtures, and accessories as well as architectural details such as doors, paneling, mantelpieces, and ceilings. These are displayed in thirty-four rooms, eighteen of which are open to visitors without appointment. The gardens surrounding Winterthur are a showy wonderland.

Close by Winterthur's sixty-four acres, the Hagley Museum shows the evolution of industry in the Brandywine Valley, a movement that affected the entire country. The museum features the growth of the Du Pont company, from gunpowder manufacturer to one of the world's largest corporations.

A prime example of the many lovely bed and breakfast homes in the Wilmington area, the one pictured here is particularly interesting because the owners have an abiding passion for mid-1950s Chevrolets. Guests are bound to see one or more in the driveway and might take time to read the popular book that these hosts put together on the subject.

WILMINGTON. Colonial stone house, built in 1940, with a manicured garden. Open year-round. Two guest rooms, shared bath. Rates: $30 to $58. Full breakfast. No children under twelve; no pets. Generally accepts only two parties who know one another. Winterthur Museum nearby. Represented by *Bed and Breakfast of Delaware, Wilmington, DE; Philadelphia Bed and Breakfast, Philadelphia, PA; Bed and Breakfast League, Ltd., Washington, DC.*

Left, the Du Pont Winterthur Museum at Wilmington. Above, the bed and breakfast's living room and upstairs guest room.

MARYLAND

Stay the night in a comfortable museum

Three and one half years of preparation went into the making of the White Swan Tavern, and the effect is that of a comfortable museum. The original section of the building dates back to the early 1700s when John Lovegrove operated a tannery on the site. Over the years the property changed hands and became a tavern that offered accommodations to travelers. In 1977, Horace Havemeyer, Jr., bought the property. Before beginning the restoration, he undertook exhaustive historical research and an archeological dig. Artifacts and shards of pottery, including a serving dish (a 1730 North Devon charger) that has been beautifully reproduced as the inn's china, are on display in a backlit wall case.

A stay at the White Swan is rewarding because guests can feel the care the inn has been given. The main floor contains three parlors, or sitting rooms. The formal and dignified Joseph Nicholson Room, named after the second owner of the property, is furnished from Mr. Nicholson's inventory, a document unearthed during research. The Isaac Cannell Room is filled with game tables appropriate to the days when it was an integral part of the original tavern.

Bedrooms are decorated in several styles. Three are done in formal colonial: one with pencil post twin beds, one with a lace canopied double bed, and one with cannonball four-posters. All have wing chairs for reading, fresh colors, and beautiful hardwood floors. The T.W. Elliason Suite, added to the tavern at the turn-of-the-century, has been restored to its Victorian origins. This bedroom and separate sitting room are decorated with high-back massive beds, a tufted settee, decorative friezes, and a busy floral carpet. A unique color scheme of golds, greens, copper, and peach is vibrant and true to the era. The final bedchamber is located in the oldest section of the structure. Named Lovegrove's Kitchen because it was the site of its namesake's tannery, this rustic suite has an original beam ceiling, brick floor, wide

Above, the old kitchen serves as a guest room.

The King Joseph Room, a private sitting room for guests, above.

In the winter the inn is filled with dried flowers.

kitchen hearth, and is accented with homespun blue-and-cream curtains and bedspreads, antique tables, and a wing chair for reading.

The White Swan's continental breakfast is special because it employs the talents of a gifted local baker and includes fresh-squeezed orange juice and grapefruit juice. Served in the Isaac Cannell Room, guests may request that breakfast be delivered to their door instead.

Chestertown, an important seaport in the early 1700s, is one of those special American towns that still reflects its moment of prosperity. The seat of Kent County and the home of Washington College, the town retains a great measure of grace and atmosphere.

WHITE SWAN TAVERN, 231 High St., Chestertown, MD 21620; (301) 778-2300; Mary S. Clarkson, hostess. Closed two weeks per year (usually early February). Five guest rooms in house, one attached "summer kitchen" suite, all private baths. Rates $65 to $75 weeknights, $75 to $90 weekends, double occupancy; $25 per extra occupant; rates include light breakfast. Good dining nearby, especially in season. Children welcome; no pets; no credit cards. Area offers local museums, walking tours, recreation, wildlife preserves.

DIRECTIONS: from Chesapeake Bay Bridge (Rte. 50-301), take Rte. 301N to Rte. 213. Turn left on Rte. 213 to Chestertown, approx. 15 miles. Cross the Chester River Bridge and turn left at first stop light (Cross St.). Turn left again at next light (High St.). Inn is in middle of block on right.

Left, above, the guests' billiard room in the contemporary townhouse. Left, below, the guest room in the historic Annapolis home, which is also shown OVERLEAF. *Above, one of a fleet of bed and breakfast boats.*

ANNAPOLIS

Living history with bed and breakfast

Annapolis resonates a quiet charm that reflects its deep sense of history. At the confluence of the Severn River and Chesapeake Bay, its setting is captivating. Narrow, crooked streets lined with brick sidewalks and old houses—more than sixty of which are pre-Revolutionary structures—lead toward the historic waterfront, where a forest of boat masts gently bob and wave. Between 1750 and 1780, Annapolis experienced its Golden Age. During those years the town built both the first library and the first theater in the colonies as well as the Maryland State House, the oldest state capitol in the United States in continuous use. It was here, too, in 1783, that General George Washington resigned his commission as commander-in-chief of the Continental Army, and, in 1784, that the Treaty of Paris was signed, officially ending the American Revolution.

The three bed and breakfast residences pictured are a varied sampler of those available in the Annapolis area. Just outside of town, one host family offers visitors the entire first floor of their contemporary townhouse, which includes a billiard room with working fireplace and color television, and an immaculate bedroom and bath. Another home, found in the center of Annapolis, is within walking distance of most of the town's historic sites and great little restaurants and bistros. As an added bonus, this house has a lovely swimming pool in its backyard.

Visitors with a nautical bent may stay aboard one of many large boats docked in the Chesapeake or downtown Annapolis.

MOTOR YACHT. Sleeps four. One of fifty motor and sailing yachts docked in downtown Annapolis, Baltimore's Inner Harbor, and the Eastern Shore that are available for bed and breakfast from April 15 to Oct. 15. Rates: 28–34 footers, $68 double, $10 third or fourth person; 35 footers and up, $75 double, $50 additional doubles (no single rate). *Represented by Sharp-Adams, Annapolis, MD.*

CONTEMPORARY TOWNHOUSE. Open year-round. One guest room, private bath, and billiard room. Rates: $40 single, $60 double. Continental breakfast, full breakfast on weekends. No children; *Represented by Sweet Dreams & Toast, Inc., Washington, DC.*

HISTORIC DISTRICT. An Annapolis "vernacular" house open year-round. One guest room, private bath. Rates for double occupancy: $56 summer, $50 winter; $5 less for singles. Full breakfast. Small pets only; smoking discouraged. *Represented by Sharp-Adams, Annapolis, MD.*

One of the restored parlors.

SPRING BANK FARM

The rebirth of a stylish rural home

In 1880 gentleman farmer George Houck spared no expense when he built the most stylish home rural Frederick County had ever seen. Constructed of red brick, the house was given a Gothic Revival bay window, columned veranda, and gabled, fish-scale patterned slate roof. It was further embellished with elegant Italianate windows and an ornate belvedere for viewing the beautiful vistas of the surrounding countryside.

A century later the house captured the imaginations of Beverly and Ray Compton, who noticed it while on a bicycle tour of the area. Captivated as well by the rich history and architectural charms of Frederick, they soon bought Spring Bank Farm and embarked on a massive and much-needed restoration. Since the Comptons open bedrooms to overnight guests as each room is completed, today's guests are attending the birth of an inn and the rebirth of a house, with such fine details as frescoed ceilings, original brass hardware, louvered shutters, hand-marbled slate fireplaces, and hand-grained woodwork revealing themselves in the process.

Ray's family has been in the antiques business for several decades, and this expertise shows in many of Spring Bank's furnishings. High-ceilinged bedrooms easily accommodate full Victorian bedroom sets, canopied beds, and easy chairs. Plans are in the works to convert the third floor, which gives access to the belvedere, into an antiques shop.

SPRING BANK FARM, 7945 Worman's Mill Rd., Frederick, MD 21701; (301) 694-0440; Beverly and Ray Compton, hosts. Elegant 1880 rural home that combines Greek Revival and Italiante architecture. Open year-round. Seven guest rooms, one with private bath. Rates $50–60 single, $60–75 double. Hearty continental breakfast. No children under twelve; no pets; no smoking in home; American Express/checks. Appalachian trail close by; trout fishing; historic district to explore. Wide range of good restaurants in town.

DIRECTIONS: from I-70, I-270, or 340, take U.S. 15 north about 5 miles, driving past Frederick. Look for "mile 16" marker; turn right at next road onto Rte. 355 south. Inn is ¼ mile south on left.

OVERLEAF: *Chesterton's First Methodist Church is an architectural gem.*

BED & BREAKFAST RESERVATION AGENCIES

The concept of Bed and Breakfast in the United States is rapidly expanding. To facilitate this phenomenon, reservation agencies are quickly cropping up, resulting in rapidly changing information. Many of the agencies listed below have been in existence for some time; others have been organized recently. Do not be surprised if there are changes when you contact them.

Connecticut

BED AND BREAKFAST, LTD., P.O. Box 216, New Haven, CT 06513; (203) 469-3260; Jack Argenio. Write or call between 5–7 P.M. weekdays and weekends. Period homes, estates, farms. *New Haven and environs.*

COVERED BRIDGE BED & BREAKFAST, West Cornwall, CT 06796; (203) 672-6052; Rae Eastman. *Northwest Connecticut, southern Berkshires.*

NUTMEG BED AND BREAKFAST, 222 Girard Avenue, Hartford, CT 06105; (203) 236-6698; Maxine Kates. 10 A.M. to 5 P.M. Monday through Friday. Vacation homes, restored historic homes. *Connecticut.*

Delaware

BED AND BREAKFAST OF DELAWARE, 1804 Breen Lane, Wilmington, DE 19810; (302) 475-0340; Barbara Rogers. *Delaware and nearby Pennsylvania and Maryland.*

District of Columbia

THE BED & BREAKFAST LEAGUE, LTD., 2855 29th Street, N.W., Washington, DC 20008; (202) 232-8718; Diana MacLeish. *U.S. and some foreign countries.*

BED 'N' BREAKFAST LTD. OF WASHINGTON, D.C., P.O. Box 12011, Washington, DC 20005; (202) 328-3510; Mila Brooks and Jackie Reed. *Mostly downtown Washington and nearby suburbs.*

SWEET DREAMS & TOAST, INC., P.O. Box 4835-0035, Washington, DC 20008; Ellie Chastain. *District of Columbia and greater Washington.*

Maine

BED AND BREAKFAST BROOKLINE/BOSTON, Box 732, Brookline, MA 02146; (617) 277-2292; Ellie Welch. 9 A.M. to 8 P.M. Victorian townhouses and Beacon Hill homes. *Boston/Brookline, Cambridge, Cape Cod, Nantucket, Martha's Vineyard.*

BED & BREAKFAST DOWN EAST LTD., Macomber Mill Road, Box 547, Eastbrook, ME 04634; (207) 565-3517; Sally Godfrey. Private homes at lakeside, countryside, town, or coast. *Maine.*

BED & BREAKFAST OF MAINE, 32 Colonial Village, Falmouth, ME 04105; (207) 781-4528; Peg Tierney. *Coastal Maine and nearby islands.*

Maryland

SHARP-ADAMS, INC., 33 West Street, Annapolis, MD 21401; (301) 269-6232, 261-2233; Cecily Sharp-Whitehill and B. J. Adams. 9 A.M. to 5 P.M. Monday through Friday. Yachts, inns, private homes. *Maryland.*

Massachusetts

BED AND BREAKFAST ASSOCIATES, Bay Colony, Ltd., P.O. Box 166, Babson Park Branch, Boston, MA 02157; (617) 449-5302; Arline Kardasis. *Eastern Massachusetts, Maine, New Hampshire, Vermont, and Connecticut.*

BED AND BREAKFAST, CAMBRIDGE AND GREATER BOSTON, 73 Kirkland Street, Cambridge, MA 02138; (617) 576-1492 or 868-4447; Riva Poor. 9 A.M. to 6 P.M. Monday–Friday; 2 P.M. to 5 P.M. Saturday and Sunday. Upper middleclass, vacation, and kosher homes. *Boston, Cambridge, Cape Cod, Martha's Vineyard, Block Island, and Nantucket.*

BED AND BREAKFAST CAPE COD, Box 341, West Hyannisport, MA 02672; (617) 775-2772; Elaine Borowick and Kay Traywick. Vacation, waterfront, historic homes. *Cape Cod.*

BERKSHIRE BED AND BREAKFAST CONNECTION, 141 Newton Road, Springfield, MA 01118; (413) 783-5111; Tim and Mary Allen. Private homes and historic places. *Central and western Massachusetts.*

HOST HOMES OF BOSTON, P.O. Box 117, Newton, MA 02168; (617) 244-1308; Marcia Whittington. *Covers suburbs in greater Boston area close to city.*

PINEAPPLE HOSPITALITY, INC., 384 Rodney French Blvd., New Bedford, MA 02744; (617) 990-1696; Joan Brownhill. 9 A.M. to 6 P.M. weekdays. Homes or small inns. *Six-state area of New England.*

Minnesota

BED AND BREAKFAST REGISTRY, P.O. Box 80174, St. Paul, MN 55108; (612) 646-4238; Mary Winget, W. Gary Winget, L. Steven Sternberg. A network of host homes, inns, and historic houses. *National.*

New Hampshire

NEW HAMPSHIRE BED & BREAKFAST, RFD 3, Box 53, Laconia, NH 03246; (603) 536-4347; Martha Dorais. Country classics, waterfront, mountain views, farms. *New Hampshire.*

New Jersey

BED AND BREAKFAST OF NEW JERSEY, Suite 132, 103 Godwin Avenue, Midland Park, NJ 07432; (201) 444-7409; Aster Mould. Vacation homes, refurbished mansions, apartments. *Northern New Jersey and seashore area.*

New York

ALTERNATE LODGINGS INC., P.O. Box 1782, East Hampton, L.I., NY 11937; (516) 324-9449; Francine and Robert Hauxwell. *The Hamptons from Westhampton to Montauk Point.*

A REASONABLE ALTERNATIVE, INC., 117 Spring Street, Port Jefferson, NY 11777; (516) 928-4034; Kathleen Dexter. Apartments, yachts, carriage houses. *Long Island.*

THE B & B GROUP (NEW YORKERS AT HOME) INC., 301 E. 60th Street, New York, NY 10022; (212) 838-7015; Farla Zammit. Host homes from brownstones to highrises. *New York City.*

BED & BREAKFAST U.S.A., LTD., 49 Van Wyck Street, Croton-on-Hudson, NY 10520; (914) 271-6228; Barbara Notarius and Ann Dantzig. *Westchester, lower Hudson Valley through Albany.*

CHERRY VALLEY VENTURES, A BED AND BREAKFAST SYSTEM, INC., 6119 Cherry Valley Turnpike, Lafayette, NY 13084; (315) 677-9723; Gloria Pallone. *Throughout New York State.*

NORTH COUNTRY BED & BREAKFAST RESERVATION SERVICE, Box 286, Lake Placid, NY 12946; (518) 523-3739; Lyn Witte. 11 A.M. to 8 P.M. daily. Private homes, country inns, and mountain resorts. *The Adirondack Mountains from Glen Falls north to the Canadian border, and from Lake Champlain west to Watertown.*

RAINBOW HOSPITALITY BED AND BREAKFAST, 9348 Hennepin Avenue, Niagara Falls, NY 14304; (716) 283-1400 or 283-0228; Marilyn Schoenherr and Gretchen Broderick. *Rochester, Niagara Falls, and Buffalo areas.*

URBAN VENTURES, INC., P.O. Box 426, New York, NY 10024; (212) 662-1234; Fran Dworan and Mary McAulay. *Manhattan and other boroughs.*

Pennsylvania

BED & BREAKFAST CENTER CITY, 1908 Spruce Street, Philadelphia, PA 19103; (215) 735-0881, 923-5459; Stella Pomerantz and Nancy Frenze. Philadelphia's *Center City, Rittenhouse Square, Antique Row, Society Hill, University City, Art Museum area.*

BED & BREAKFAST IN LANCASTER, HARRISBURG, AND HERSHEY AREAS, 463 North Market Street, Elizabethtown, PA 17022; (717) 367-9408; Judy Snavely. Call evenings.

BED & BREAKFAST OF PHILADELPHIA, P.O. Box 680, Devon, PA 19333; (215) 688-1633; Sandra Fullerton, Joanne Goins, Carol Yarrow. *Philadelphia, its suburbs, and surrounding historic countryside, including Valley Forge, Doylestown, and New Hope.*

PITTSBURGH BED & BREAKFAST, Box 25353, Pittsburgh, PA 15242; (412) 241-5746; Karen Krull.

BED AND BREAKFAST POCONO NORTHEAST, P.O. Box 115, Bear Creek, PA 18602; (717) 472-3145; Patricia Mack and Ann Magagna. 9 A.M. to noon; also evenings except Tuesday. Private homes and historic houses. *Northeast Pennsylvania, including the Poconos.*

BED & BREAKFAST OF SOUTHEAST PENNSYLVANIA, Box 278, R.D. 1, Barto, PA 19504; (215) 845-3526; Joyce Stevenson. Call anytime. Old farmhouses, restored grist mills, town and suburban houses. *Lehigh, Northampton, Berkshire, and Western Bucks counties.*

COUNTRY COUSINS BED & BREAKFAST REGISTRY, 228 West Main Street, Waynesboro, PA 17268; (717) 762-2722; Karen Bercaw. 1 P.M. to 6 P.M. weekdays. *South central Pennsylvania from the Susquehanna to Bedford and eastern West Virginia.*

REST & REPAST BED & BREAKFAST SERVICE, P.O. Box 126, Pine Grove Mills, PA 16868; (814) 238-1484; Linda Feltman and Brent Peters. After 5 P.M. weekdays; anytime Saturday or Sunday. Farms, National Historic Register homes, apartments. *Penn State vicinity.*

Rhode Island

CASTLE KEEP, 44 Everett Street, Newport, RI 02840; (401) 846-0362; Audrey Grimes and Dorothy Ranhofer. 8 A.M. to 8 P.M. Restored colonials, Victorian minimansions, and condos by the sea.

GUEST HOUSE ASSOCIATION OF NEWPORT, 23 Brinley Street, Newport, RI 02840; (401) 849-7645; George Van Duinwyk, President of the Association.

Vermont

VERMONT BED & BREAKFAST, Box 139, Browns Trace, Jericho, VT 05465; (802) 899-2354; Sue and Dave Eaton, Sheila and Todd Varnum. *Vermont only.*